BOB

By Pamela Trescott and Chuck Ashman

Kissinger – The Adventures of Super Kraut
Martha Mitchell – The Mouth That Roared
The Adventures of Big Bad John Connally
The CIA-Mafia Link
The Strange Disappearance of Jimmy Hoffa
The Finest Judges Money Can Buy
The Gospel According to Billy Graham
Outrage – The Abuse of Diplomatic Immunity
Cary Grant

BOB HOPE
A Comic Life

Pamela Trescott

A STAR BOOK

published by

the Paperback Division of
W. H. Allen & Co. PLC

A Star Book
Published in 1988
by the Paperback Division of
W. H. Allen & Co. PLC
44 Hill Street, London W1X 8LB

First published in Great Britain by
W. H. Allen & Co. PLC, 1987

Printed in Great Britain by
Cox & Wyman Ltd, Reading

ISBN 0 352 32197 0

1

Growing Up the Hard Way

As the last decade of the twentieth century approaches, it's hard to picture what life was like nearly a hundred years ago. The 'Gay Nineties', when 'gay' meant nothing more than happy and glad, was an exciting time to be alive. Inventors had only recently given the world such marvellous innovations as the telephone, the telegraph, and the gramophone. The next century would see new ideas and inventions bring change at a rate often too rapid to take in, but then it was all just getting started.

La Belle Epoque. The Gay Nineties. Mankind's future had never looked brighter. Art and music flourished. Women looked elegant in pompadour hair-do's. The sun still hadn't set on the British Empire, and Britain ruled the waves as well as her colonies and protectorates around the world. Victoria was still the queen, although she, too, was nearing the end of a long, influential reign.

For ordinary folk, life didn't exactly mirror the popular image of drawing rooms and elegant carriages, but it wasn't necessarily bad either. It wasn't bad at all if you were a master craftsman, skilled in construction and stonemasonry. Such a man was James Hope, an artisan who a few years earlier had gone to Paris to help carve the Statue of Liberty.

James Hope and his wife had nine children – seven sons and two daughters. They lived at Weston-super-Mare, but James and his sons, who were skilled workmen, often spent long weeks at construction sites far afield. One of those sons, William Henry, known as 'Harry', was also a stonemason. A well-built, muscular, good-looking young man, he was good at his craft and had dreams of becoming an architect.

Near the end of 1890, Harry went across the Bristol Channel

with his father to help build new stone docks in Barry, Wales. The young man was almost 21 years old.

Living in Barry at that time was a young girl named Avis Towns.* Avis was a 15-year-old orphan. Described as fragile-looking, with Dresden china-doll features, Avis had lost her handsome, well-travelled parents in a shipwreck when she was barely old enough to know them. She was being raised in a foster home, the home of a retired sea-captain named Lloyd, and the family were good to her. Music was one of her favourite pastimes; she sang and had learned to play several instruments. But musical activities and the kindness of the Lloyd family were not enough to fill her life, and she was lonely.

When Avis saw young Harry Hope working on the docks, she stopped and stared. She started coming back every day. Harry noticed her, too. Soon they had talked, probably flirted together, and before long had fallen in love.

Harry's father, James, was not particularly pleased. Flirting boys did not get much work done. He told Harry he was moving him to another site. Before leaving, Harry searched for Avis around the docks to tell her. When they finally caught sight of each other, and Harry told her the bad news, Avis collapsed to the ground. Harry ran to her, picked up the slight form, and placed her in his father's arms. He informed James that he wanted to marry this girl.

James said, 'But she is just a baby.' Whereupon the young lady in question, apparently unconscious in his arms, suddenly opened her eyes and declared that she was in fact a woman. James set her on her feet and told young Harry to marry her.

The two young people were married in Cardiff on 25 April 1891. One can only suppose that they shared the hopes of most newly-weds: a healthy, happy family and comfortable means. One doubts that they ever expected that one of their children would become one of the most celebrated, well-loved and richest men in the world. But young candidates for such glory, children to hope and dream for, soon began to arrive and over the next twelve years, the family steadily grew. Unfortunately, their fortunes did not.

* This is the correct British spelling according to family records. The 'e' in Townes was added by immigration officials in the USA.

The first-born was Ivor; then came James Francis II and then, a joy to both parents, a daughter, Emily. She was followed by Frederick Charles. Before their next son, William John, was born, precious little Emily died of diphtheria, as did so many children in those days. It was a time of sadness for the Hopes.

The young family did well at first, but before long, it became more difficult for Harry to support them. They moved, first from Newport, Monmouthshire, back to Barry, then to Lewisham, in London. After they left Barry the last time, Avis neither saw nor heard from her foster parents, the Lloyds, again. Her lot was truly set with her husband and her children. In Lewisham, Harry began having trouble finding work. The search for work brought them first to Kent and then to 44 Creighton Road in Eltham, a row house built by Grandfather James.

This was to be the birthplace of a little mite who would grow up to entertain the world – who would help America laugh through a Depression and three wars, who would dine with Presidents and royalty, who would master the stage, radio, television and movies. To have guessed all this at the time, one would have had to be Merlin, who lived backwards through time; or perhaps the most imaginative science fiction writer who ever lived, because radio, television and movies were then barely concepts in the minds of unique dreamers.

The rash of inventions and technological breakthroughs that would characterize the twentieth century had only just begun in the decade of the Gay Nineties. These innovations would soon affect both entertainment and communications as well as life-styles generally.

In 1891, Thomas Edison took out his first patent on a motion picture camera, a device perfected by the Lumière brothers just a few years later. The zipper was invented and rayon (viscose), the first man-made fibre, was discovered. Mr Diesel patented the internal combustion engine and Henry Ford built his first car. Henri Toulouse-Lautrec produced his first music-hall posters, Conan Doyle published 'The Adventures of Sherlock Holmes' in *Strand* magazine, Gauguin settled in Tahiti and Herman Melville, the author of *Moby Dick*, passed away. Not to be ignored in a book about the 'old duffer', the first US Open Golf Championship was held in 1895.

Other events in the world were affecting not only the future but the present. Queen Victoria, who ruled during what has been described as the golden age of British architecture, died in 1901. Demand for skilled stonemasons dropped sharply as people turned to the more inexpensive, although less attractive, brick. Bricklayers moved up in the world of the building trades, the artisans like Harry Hope suffered. Work became harder and harder for them to find.

Harry began to find solace at the local pubs. He fell prey to 'friends' who convinced him to invest his savings in scams. Sometimes he took his troubles to other women. But for all his human frailties, Harry was really devoted to Avis and his family. In his depression over lack of work, he often spent too much time at the local ale-house, but he would come home to Avis with a bouquet of flowers in his hands. She would wait up for him. They might have had fights, but Harry and Avis loved each other.

Avis was pregnant again. On 29 May 1903, she didn't feel well. It was too early for the baby, so she decided it was just a bit of the flu. She went about her daily work, managing her four rumbustious boys and even scrubbing the floor. Harry, as usual, went to the pub. Finally Avis felt so bad that she went to bed and sent one of the boys for the doctor. The doctor was told to come in the back door because of the newly scrubbed floors. He sized up the situation immediately, and before long, Avis and Harry's fifth son was born. The boy was in a hurry to come into the world.

They named him Leslie Towns Hope – Leslie for a famous soccer hero of the day, and Towns for Avis' long-dead parents.

Many years were to pass before Leslie would change his name to Bob (which he considered 'chummier'), and eventually would find himself entertaining at the White House in Washington, DC, pointing out what a red-letter year he had chosen to be born in.

The year 1903 saw not only the birth of this famous entertainer, but:

- the first successful flight of a powered aeroplane by the Wright brothers
- the creation of the 'Teddy' bear (named for Teddy Roosevelt)
- the production of the longest film to date, *The Great Train Robbery*, which ran a full twelve minutes
- the invention of the electrocardiograph
- the founding of the Bolshevik party in London by Lenin and Trotsky

- the laying of the first Pacific cable between San Francisco and Manila
- the first cross-country auto drive in the US. (It took 52 days.)
- the establishment of a 20 mph speed limit for motorcars in England
- the founding of the Ford Motor Company.

For Leslie Hope, there were more personally important events which occurred over the next three years as he toddled around in his nappies under the watchful eye of Avis and his older brothers. The first radio transmission of music took place in 1904; in 1905, the first regular cinema was established in Pittsburgh, Pennsylvania, and the first neon lights went up; and in 1906, the first radio programme combining both voice and music was broadcast.

Soon after little Leslie's birth, the Hope family moved again, first to one, and then another, cheaper house in Weston-super-Mare where Harry had grown up. The Boer War had just ended and times were even tougher. There was almost no work for Harry. The stone quarries were closed up. Poverty was everywhere. The older boys and even Avis went to work. Avis was a cashier in a tea shop, and her baby, Leslie, went with her to work.

In 1905, Harry broke his ankle and couldn't work at all. The boys continued to earn what money they could. Finally, they moved to Bristol in hopes that Harry could find employment there when his ankle healed. (Coincidentally, Bristol was also then the home of a young boy named Archie Leach, just a few months younger than Leslie Hope. Little Archie would later grow up to become Cary Grant.)

The family's finances didn't improve much in Bristol. And there was yet another mouth to feed with the birth of Avis and Harry's sixth son, Sidney. Still hoping to find a better means of supporting his family, Harry Hope began to pay more attention to the letters coming from two of his brothers, Frank and Fred, who had gone to America to seek their fortunes. They had settled in Cleveland, Ohio, and sent home glowing reports of the opportunities there. They told Harry that there was still plenty of work for stonemasons in the US and encouraged him to join them. Harry looked at the job situation in Bristol and decided it couldn't be worse in America. He decided to emigrate.

Harry decided that the best thing to do was to go over by himself and get things going before bringing Avis and the boys over. Life remained hard for them in Bristol after Harry left. The older boys continued to work at whatever they could find and Avis worked hard to keep the family in good spirits. She had some help from little Leslie, who early on showed definite signs of having a natural gift for comedy. He was reportedly a mimic at the tender age of four, a tiny jester who used to make his aged Aunt Polly, a woman of 102 years, laugh. He earned a cookie for his efforts.

Harry's letters to Avis showed him to be a happy man. It seems that Cleveland was everything he had expected. When at last he wrote that it was time for his family to join him, the first problem was to find the money for passage. It was Christmas, 1907. In 1904, steerage rates for immigrants to the United States had been cut to $10 by foreign lines, but it was still a good bit of money for the large family to raise. Avis cut back on the family's use of fuel that cold winter to try to save money, and the boys continued to work. But it was not enough. Finally, Avis was forced to sell her treasured spinet and the grandfather clock from Scotland that she loved so well.

With tearful good-byes to their relatives, the family finally set off. It was not an easy trip. They took two steerage cabins, each hot and noisy. After her gold watch was stolen out of her cabin the first night, Avis moved the whole family into one cabin for safety. At last they arrived in New York, to find a heavy fog shrouding Ellis Island and only the Statue of Liberty, on which the boys' grandfather had worked, to greet them. They still faced a long, difficult overland journey to Cleveland, where Harry would be waiting for them.

Avis straightened her spine once again and marshalled her brood through the immigration procedures and off to the train to Cleveland. With few toilet facilities and minimal food, the trip seemed endless. Avis, the eternal morale booster, led the boys in singing to pass the trip. Everyone was anxious to see Harry again.

At last the long journey was over. Harry and the uncles met them and there were hugs all around. Their first stop was Uncle Frank's and Aunt Louisa's, a small apartment they all crowded into for a few days. Before long, Avis rented a small, church-owned house for the family on Euclid Avenue.

One of the first things Avis and the children saw in Cleveland was the Newkland Avenue Presbyterian Church, which Harry had helped to build. Although they were Episcopalian when they arrived, they soon began attending the new Presbyterian Church. Harry, though, was not really a reformed man. He still drank a great deal and was unable to find regular and steady employment. His reports back to Bristol had been exaggerated; in fact the older boys continued to have to work just to meet the family's rent. There was a financial panic in the country, Harry's skills were now going out of vogue in America as they had in Great Britain, and life was particularly difficult for immigrants.

Before long, Avis packed up the family again and moved them to a larger house where she took in boarders. The fragile little girl who swooned on the docks in Barry had become a woman of great strength and determination who did whatever she had to do to keep her beloved family together.

A year after they arrived in Cleveland, the seventh and last Hope child was born. George Percy was the first American citizen in the family. The family rallied round. Before long, Harry was eligible for citizenship. Upon Harry's naturalization, the entire Hope family became Americans.

Harry still seemed to have a problem with drinking, but for all that, he remained a devoted husband and father – a romantic with Avis and a man whose interest in his sons never flagged.

Leslie joined in his family's industriousness and took up selling newspapers. Bob Hope likes to tell the story of one memorable sale. The boys became accustomed to a large, black limousine coming to their street corner, with an arm reaching out with two cents to buy the paper. The arm belonged to John D. Rockefeller, whose name was a household word for wealth and success. One day, when Leslie still didn't know who was in the car, it stopped, and the man proffered a dime. Leslie had no change, so he told the man that he could wait and pay him the next day. The man leaned out and said, 'Young man, I'm going to give you some advice. If you want to be a success in business, trust nobody – never give credit and always keep change in hand. That way you won't miss any customers going for it.' Leslie indeed thought of the customers he was missing as he went to fetch Mr Rockefeller's eight cents change. But he remembered the encounter for a long, long time.

Leslie Hope also had to go to school. Puns on his name gave him the nicknames 'Hopelessly' and 'Hopeless'. These names prompted his early career of scrapping. The poor boy from the hard streets of Bristol was quite capable of defending himself.

Academics were not Hope's strong suit. Where he shone was in music, following in his mother's footsteps, and in athletic activity, although not necessarily the organized kind. Going to the movies was also a favourite pastime. (In 1912, when Les Hope was nine years old, a reported 5,000,000 people per *day* attended US movie theatres.)

Les' best friend was a boy named Whitey, and the pair, along with Les' brothers Jack and Sidney, engaged in all three activities – sometimes to the dismay of those around them.

It was necessary for the Hope boys to earn their own money if they expected to have any for themselves, as well as make a much-needed contribution to the family funds. Les' two main ways of earning money did not always include regular part-time jobs. He had a beautiful voice, and with his pal and his two brothers, would sing on street corners and in streetcars. He would frequently solo. Afterwards, the boys would pass the hat.

The gang were also fast on their feet. They would wangle their way into company picnic footraces. Their strategy for winning often included more than just running hard.

Prizes for the races used to be five dollars for first place and three dollars for second place. The boys would win everything by using a clever, if not entirely ethical, trick. The trick was that if someone else, outside the gang, appeared to be very fast, one of the gang would stumble during the race to put the speeder off his stride. Then Leslie or Whitey would race ahead and win the prize.

Les also spent some time in pool halls and engaged in other less-than-respectable activities. The crowning point of his mis-behaviour was probably when he was arrested and put in jail.

He was arrested for stealing. The loot was tennis racquets and balls. The gang was caught a few hours after the heist, playing tennis in a parking lot. Hope was put in the 'slammer' and scared out of his wits until collected by his far from pleased parents. He was forced to promise to shape up. He did, and never went back on his word. But like he tells it, he never had a 'real' job either. Aside from a series of part-time, temporary jobs, Leslie Towns Hope was made for show business.

Although Hope's youth was very poor, much of the responsi-bility for the family's welfare fell on the shoulders of his older brothers. They helped make it easier for Les to take life a little less seriously. But the impact of his circumstances didn't escape him.

His mother's values of hard work and good cheer would stay with him throughout his life. And work he did. Some of his jobs included: delivery boy for a baker; soda jerk; butcher's assistant; shoe salesman; caddy at a golf club; and clerk in a flower stall. However, nothing seemed to strike his fancy quite like the movies.

In 1909, D. W. Griffith had featured Mary Pickford, 'America's sweetheart', as the first movie star. By 1914, the great Charlie Chaplin was making one movie after another. Les was a great movie fan. Charlie Chaplin was his idol. He never missed a picture and was always amazed at how much laughter the little man could evoke.

In 1915, there was a fad for holding Charlie Chaplin look-alike contests. Les Hope had been imitating the 'Little Tramp' for his family and friends. The gang encouraged him to enter one of the contests in Luna Park, then packed the audience, which clapped so hard for him that he won. There was enough prize money to buy Avis a new cooker.

Courtesy of the pool hall, Les and Whitey also made friends with two boys named Charlie Cooley and Johnny Gibbons, who had a fun sideline to pool-hustling. They were dancers – tap and speciality. They taught Les how to dance, how to box, and how to be very good at pool hustling.

Les Hope dropped out of high school when he became a sophomore, which was as soon as the law allowed. Life on the streets was much more exciting and, apparently, profitable.

Les and Whitey continued to work the pool halls, and they would sing from time to time and pass the hat. They began to think about performing as a career. Like most teenagers, though, they had more than one idea about what they wanted to be when they grew up. For a while, it looked like boxing might win out.

Whitey entered an amateur match under the name of Packy West (after the legendary Packy McFarland). Les decided he could do anything Whitey could do, so he signed up for the fight as Packy East.

He actually won his first bout. His second fight was against a boy named Happy Walsh who later became a local champion. Happy quite happily put 'Packy East' out of the fight business.

The year 1920 approached, the age of the flapper. Les Hope would be 17 years old. The Great War, the 'War to End All Wars', had been fought and the armistice signed in 1918. The world had seen the first commercial manufacture of plastic; a woman in London had received the first permanent wave and 'bobs' were all the rage; on Hope's fourteenth birthday in 1917, a quiet event had occurred that would eventually change the world: the birth of John Fitzgerald Kennedy; Ziegfeld's Follies had been dancing for a decade; and on 16 January 1919 the constitutional amendment requiring prohibition of alcoholic beverages in America had been ratified (it would go into effect the next year).

Nineteen hundred and twenty was also the year in which Les Hope definitely made up his mind to become an entertainer. That same year, Westinghouse began the first American broadcasting station in Pittsburgh, Pennsylvania, and the first sound film experiments had recently occurred. What auspicious timing!

Les knew that his dancing needed work, so he sought out a man by the name of King Rastus Brown for lessons. Meanwhile he supported himself by working for his brother, Fred, who had a meat stand. Les' friend Johnny Gibbons was his co-worker, and the two used to cut antics a great deal more than they cut steaks and chops. Fred would get exasperated, but he also admitted that the pair were funny.

Fred later was to marry Johnny's sister, and Les also fell in love for the first time in his life. The girl was Mildred Rosequist. They met at a party, and Les thought she danced better than Irene Castle. Mildred worked at a department store. Eventually, her blonde good looks got her a job as a fashion model for the store.

The two became serious about each other, although Mildred's mother viewed the whole business with extreme dismay. Les couldn't keep a regular job. The two spent much of their time together dancing. They wanted to go professional, to be the next Nick and Irene Castle. They practised far into the night, every night, usually to the phonograph in the kitchen after everyone else had gone to bed. Les even bought her an engagement ring, rumoured to be the smallest rock in all of Cleveland.

Eventually, Les decided he had no more to learn from King Rastus Brown, and he and Mildred signed up with an old vaudevillian named Johnny Root who taught at a place called Sojack's Dance Academy. There the young couple took enough lessons to be able to put together what would be Les Hope's first professional act.

2

A 'Dancemedian'

When Leslie and Mildred first hit the boards they didn't exactly take Cleveland by storm, but they survived. Their first paid job was for three nights at a social club located in the Brotherhood of Engineers Building, where they danced between other acts as a kind of intermission entertainment. They did well and began to get other engagements. Generally, these were performances in movie theatres, either as the intermission act or as part of a vaudeville review accompanying a movie. Movies were silent, so with the piano player and the old theatre stages that were used, it was natural to have live entertainment adding to the images on the flickering screen.

It is not clear from their later recollections exactly what was the professional status of the two young performers. Mildred thought that they were doing benefits, but she has said that in later years, Bob Hope frequently told people that they had been paid $7 or $8 per performance and had split it between them. Whether or not they were actually paid, Mildred herself did not recall receiving any money.

The young lovers began to plan their professional and personal future together. They dreamed of going on the road together – joining up with some small vaudeville circuit. It was not to be, however.

Mrs Rosequist, Mildred's mother, considered Leslie Hope on about the same level as a snail. He didn't seem to be able to keep a job and he was, perhaps, a little too smooth. Her daughter would certainly not be allowed to go on the road with him without a chaperone and there was no chaperone available. She herself was not going to do it.

At Sojack's Dance Academy, Johnny Root was getting ready to

close down. Hope decided to take over the school, confident that he could make a go of it. His business card read: 'LESLIE T. HOPE WILL TEACH YOU HOW TO DANCE – BUCK AND WING, ECCENTRIC, WALTZ-CLOG AND SOFT SHOE.' Unfortunately, he was no more successful than Root had been, and the school soon went bankrupt.

After being fired from another part-time job, Hope began to think seriously about taking a vaudeville act on the road. It was obvious that Mildred would not be allowed to join him, so he started looking around for another partner. He found him in Lloyd 'Lefty' Durbin, an old pal from the neighbourhood. The two practised an act that included a little tap dancing, a little soft shoe, and a little 'eccentric' dancing, the kind that would get a laugh. They worked amateur contests and small vaudeville houses around Cleveland, often packing the audience with their friends and family.

Eventually, they got an agent who booked them into a place called the Bandbox. The headliner for the show was Fatty Arbuckle. The year was 1924. Arbuckle had been one of the fledgling movie industry's first stars, beginning as an extra in 1903, and by 1916 was writing, directing and acting in his own films. He gave Buster Keaton his first part. But in 1921, at the peak of his success, Arbuckle was ruined by a scandal. At a party he gave in San Francisco, where there was a great deal of drinking, the fiancée of one of Arbuckle's directors went into severe convulsions. This occurred after she had allegedly been the victim of a perverted sexual assault by the 320-pound actor. The woman died a few days later of a ruptured bladder, and Arbuckle was charged with manslaughter. His first two trials ended in hung juries and in the third trial, he was acquitted. Arbuckle's career was in ruins, however, due to the treatment of the case by the press and the general moral indignation of the public, who were appalled by the allegations about a den of iniquity in moviedom.* His films were banned and withdrawn from circulation.

In 1925, Fatty Arbuckle managed to return to Hollywood as director using the pseudonym William B. Goodrich. However, when Les Hope and Lefty Durbin joined his show in 1924, he

---

* This case led to the formation of the famous Hays Office which effectively censored the film industry for many years to come.

was still being forced to work in small-time, out-of-the-way vaudeville houses.

As their first act, Les and Lefty spoofed an Egyptian dance. Arbuckle thought they were great. The show closed before very long, but it was their lucky break. Arbuckle still had a lot of friends in show business, and he introduced the boys to a producer of tabloid shows. 'Tabs' were all the rage in small-time vaudeville shows. They were essentially miniature musical-comedies.

Les and Lefty were hired for a tab called 'Jolly Follies' which played the Gus Sun circuit. The boys joined it in East Palestine, Ohio, as members of the chorus. By Thanksgiving of 1924, the show was in Bloomington, Indiana, and Les Hope got his first chance to actually speak to the audience when he filled in for the ailing MC (Master of Ceremonies) of one of the sketches.

'Frankly', the lead singer of the 'Follies', Hazel Chamberlain, later recalled, 'we had all thought Lefty Durbin was the more likely of the two to be a comic, but that night Les Hope was as much surprised as the rest of us.'[1]

Hope was pretty impressed with himself, too, after this success. He was doing what he really wanted to do. He had found that he loved travelling, and loved being in front of an audience. His loud applause reinforced that feeling. Whenever the show returned to Cleveland, Hope loved to play it up to family and friends. His first stop in Cleveland was always Mildred's house, where he continued to receive a warm welcome. Even Mrs Rosequist began to think he might be starting to make something of himself. Not so at home, however. Les' family thought he was merely going through a 'phase'. They expected him to come home one day, get a 'real' job, and marry Mildred.

Les was now earning $40 per week. Half of it went to Avis to help with the family expenses, and he lived off the rest. Life on the small-time vaudeville circuit was less than wonderful for anyone who didn't have stars in their eyes. The theatres were ill-equipped, with tiny backstage areas. The boarding houses were often cramped and cold, with limited sanitary facilities. But for Les Hope and Lefty Durbin, the smell of greasepaint overwhelmed any of the less desirable odours on the tour and kept them happy.

Hope's enthusiasm was reinforced by a crush on one of the troupe members, a lovely young pianist named Kathleen O'Shea.

Mildred wasn't out of the picture, but she told him she too was going to date other people. One night, he was in Kathleen's hotel room with his shirt off. Apparently, Kathleen was putting hot salve on his congested chest, but when the hotel manager came to the door and demanded to know what was going on, he didn't listen to the explanation. He pointed a gun at the stuttering young Hope and ordered him downstairs. Hotels insisted on high moral standards from the entertainment troupes staying with them. In fact, many hotels at that time refused even to admit performers.

While their life on the road suited Les perfectly, it didn't suit his partner. Lefty had never looked particularly healthy, and now the rigours of poor food, draughty rooms, and an unsettled life seemed to catch up with him. On a small stage in Huntington, West Virginia, he collapsed. After he bled from the mouth, bad food was blamed for his condition. Lefty continued to get worse, and Les decided to take him home to Cleveland.

Lefty might easily have had a case of food poisoning, but the real problem turned out to be consumption. Consumption was then the common term for tuberculosis, and in fact many people contracted tuberculosis in those days.

Lefty lost a lot of blood and was in a weakened condition. He had probably been sick for a long time. Three days after returning to Cleveland, he died.

A dejected Les made his way back to the 'Jolly Follies' to find that a new partner had been hired for him. The two went to work immediately, practising together and becoming a team. The new partner, George Byrne, was a good dancer as well as a good man. The two soon became friends, and Byrne's sister later married Hope's brother, George.

Hope and Byrne, as the billing went, were a success. They got great reviews which led, as so often happens, to a certain amount of dissatisfaction. They wanted to do more. They wanted to use their voices and not just their dancing feet.

Hope was now known as 'Lester' Hope, thinking it sounded more masculine than Leslie. 'Lester' got a chance from time to time to fill in as a tenor in some four-part harmony acts with the show.

Hope and Byrne continued on the circuit through 1926. From time to time, they would get a little time off, and usually spent their holidays at the Hope home in Cleveland, relaxing, rehearsing new moves, and gorging themselves on Avis' cooking. Hope and Mildred continued to be an 'item', dancing together and engaging in romance on her front porch. (Kathleen had left the show to open a dress shop in Morgantown.)

Hope and Byrne eventually realized that if they wanted to do more than dance, they were going to have to leave the Gus Sun circuit. They quit in the spring of 1926 and took themselves to Detroit, where they knew an agent named Ted Snow. Snow got them a booking for a whopping $175 a week, a great deal more than they had been making, and also found them a late-night spot in a nightclub for extra money.

Hope watched the MC in his new show very carefully. The man used current events in his comedy routines, which went over very well with the audience. Hope listened and learned.

The boys were getting good reviews booked as the 'Dancing Demons'. They had new costumes and good publicity. From Detroit, they went to Pittsburgh, equipped now with professional photographs. In Pittsburgh, they worked up an act they thought good enough for New York City, the dream venue of all vaudevillians of the time. New York was the home of Broadway, and of all the big ruling dynasties of the entertainment world like the Ziegfelds, the Hammersteins and the Loews. The biggest stars played New York, and the acts that hoped to make the big time went there to be close to the action and attempt to be noticed.

Hope and Byrne got no warmer welcome than other inexperienced young hopefuls, but their publicity photographs finally got them noticed at the powerful William Morris Agency. They were booked into an act on the famous Keith Circuit, performing in what has to be one of the strangest routines in Hope's long career. Hope and Byrne were the dancing partners of Daisy and Violet Hilton, a pair of Siamese twins who had been performing since they were children. They had a long act, which ended with them dancing back to back with our two heroes. It was well-received and the novelty of it packed the houses. Hope and Byrne also had their own act in the show. They played the Circuit for six months, travelling around the East Coast.

The boys were now booking themselves as 'Dancemedians', building humour into their act. They were well received by local critics at their stops.

By the time they got to Providence, Rhode Island, the boys were tired. They were working long hours, doing not only their own act, but performing twice in each show with the Hilton sisters. They demanded more money. It was refused, so they packed their trunk and left the show. The year was 1927.

After a little while doing brief nightclub dates, they finally struck it rich in August when they were cast in 'The Sidewalks of New York'. Some of the top vaudevillians of the day were in this show, and although Hope and Byrne's part was small, only a little speciality dancing, they were in heady company.

Hope's eye was captured by a young lady named Barbara Sykes, an aspiring actress. Mildred was still in his heart, but as time went by, there was enough room for others as well. The affair, such as it was, didn't last long. Barbara fell in love with a piano player, whom she married while Hope was away in out-of-town try-outs.

More important than romantic disappointments, or anything else, was the fact that the boys were in a hit show. The headliners were Ruby Keeler and her romantic partner, Al Jolson. Despite the enormous competition in New York at that time, both the audiences and the critics loved 'The Sidewalks of New York'.

The good times didn't last long, though. The director decided there were too many dancers in the show, and gave Hope and Byrne their notice.

Fortunately, it didn't take long for them to get into another Broadway show. And this time they were more than just boys in the chorus. Unfortunately, they were a bomb. It was time to rethink their position.

Taking a series of minor bookings, they worked their way back to Cleveland, where they arrived by Christmas. On the way, they made the hard decision to break up the act. Byrne thought Hope could do better on his own.

Hope stayed in Cleveland for a while, living at home, and getting himself his first job as a single act working theatres in Cleveland. He started off in blackface, but soon dropped the makeup, relying on a tilt of the chin or a wink of the eye to deliver the joke.

Later in 1927, Hope set off for Chicago to try for bookings at more prestigious theatres than could be found in Cleveland. Nothing happened. He went from agent to agent, theatre to theatre, trying for any booking he could get. By mid-year he knew he was defeated. Penniless and depressed, he had just about made up his mind to go home.

Just when he was at rock bottom, Hope had a major stroke of luck. He ran into his old friend, Charlie Cooley. Charlie was a successful vaudevillian who had grown up with Hope back in the old neighbourhood. He used his influence and got Leslie a booking through an agent named Charles Hogan.

Hope's job was as an MC for three shows on Decoration Day for $25. He was good enough to get another booking at the Stratford, a neighbourhood theatre, for three days. Again, he was an MC. His performance was good enough to ensure a new deal for two weeks, which was later stretched to four weeks at $200 a week.

Once again, Hope was able to pay his rent, eat and keep body and soul together.

At this time Leslie Hope, or Lester Hope as he was now calling himself, decided to change his name to Bob. He thought it was 'chummier' and that it looked better on a marquee. No doubt he was right.

Hope's act combined comedy and singing. He soon realized he needed a steady supply of fresh jokes to keep the audience interested, as they returned to see his act time and time again. He used joke books, and occasionally begged jokes from other acts. Often, he'd write an original gag. One of the better gags began with an off-stage crash. Hope would emerge from the wings, wipe his hands and adjust his clothes as though he had just been in a fight. He'd look back towards the curtains and sneer, 'Lie there and bleed.' The audience loved it.

Hope's four-week booking at the Stratford Theatre eventually turned into six months. In addition to prompting his name change, this booking in effect gave birth to the Bob Hope that the whole world has learned to love. This regular work helped him develop the comedy style that would stay with him to the present day.

What he did was to quickly and flatly tell his joke – and then wait. He'd stare at the audience, waiting quietly, until they got the joke and the laughter came. With pacing and timing, he learned to control his audience.

At the Stratford, Hope experimented with routines. He learned to judge his audience and adjust to what they thought was funny.

In Chicago at the Stratford, Bob Hope was probably in as good a position as he had ever been. Regular money, regular meals, and the good feeling that comes from being successful put a healthy glow in his cheeks and a spring in his step. What's more, he was in love once again.

This time, the lady was Louise Troxell. Louise was a secretary, but she was stage-struck. She was a very attractive, sophisticated-looking young woman. The two soon became an 'item'.

In October, 1928, Hope felt it was time for a change of pace. He decided to leave the Stratford and hit the road again. This time, he asked Louise to be his partner.

Hope's idea was similar to the one George Burns had had when he teamed up with Gracie Allen, although the result was different. When Gracie joined George on stage, she turned out to be the funnier of the two and George played her straight man. With Bob Hope and Louise Troxell, Louise played it straight, and also served as a set-decoration.

She was a beautiful girl, and the act worked. Hope and Louise played several houses on the Keith Circuit in the Mid-West.

When 1929 rolled around, Hope was back at the Stratford for another six months. He became desperate for new material, and found himself actually lifting material from other comics, a fairly common practice at the time. Despite doing everything possible to get fresh material, Hope could not find enough, and decided it would be better to go back on the road. There one could find fresh audiences for old material – a much easier task.

He and Louise took off again. This time, Hope had star billing in the show, for the first time ever. Soon he was making $325 a week. He gave Louise pocket money and sent Avis about $50 a week. On this run, he learned even more about timing and judging audiences, and he learned to adjust his act to accommodate Texas audiences accustomed to a much slower delivery than he had used in the North.

The manager of this circuit was so impressed with Hope and his act that he sent a telegram to the Keith office in New York stating that he thought the young man would do well on the more prestigious Orpheum circuit.*

The suggestion was accepted and Hope and Louise were invited to New York. Perhaps invitation is not exactly the right

* Radio-Keith-Orpheum is what RKO, the big movie studio in later years, was named after.

word, though. There was no job waiting for them. In fact, Hope had to scramble just to find a minor booking to serve as a showcase so the producers could see his act. Through a combination of *chutzpah* and bravado, he managed to pull it off. He was good enough in the showcase to be called back for several bows and even an encore.

Hope was offered a contract on the Orpheum Circuit for $400 a week. With sheer brass, he told the producers it wasn't enough. He finally accepted $450 per week for three years. He was aiming for New York's Palace, the pinnacle of vaudeville.

The time was October, 1929. It was the beginning of one of the most difficult periods of American history. The stock market crashed. The giddy sense of riding high that had gripped so much of the public for so long was quick to fade as the grim realities of the Great Depression set in.

After the crash, it took some time for the impact of the disaster to be felt. In the short term, the problem seemed to belong to Wall Street brokers and some investors. It was weeks before the sad truth of the Depression's widespread effect began to be recognized.

In the meantime, and surely afterwards, people needed more than ever to be entertained. Vaudeville as an industry was more concerned about the inroads the new talking pictures were making into their audiences than anything else. This fear of encroachment by a new type of entertainment upon an older one's audience is common. Following the growth of the movie industry, the arrival of television caused great worry to the movie-makers, and most recently, the videocassette 'revolution' has come on the scene to strike fear in the hearts of movie, broadcast and cable TV executives alike. In these latter cases, some readjustments were necessary, but the predicted disasters have never come. The different forms of entertainment all remain available, and, with some periodic ups and downs, all are thriving.

Vaudeville, though, did have good reason to worry. The arrival of the 'talkies' was indeed the beginning of the end for vaudeville. It could be argued that it continues to this day in variety shows and programmes like the Bob Hope specials, but the old-style vaudeville of pack-your-trunk and travel from place to place with novelty acts has died out.

Bob Hope didn't believe it could happen at first. He was close to reaching the top of an industry that had occupied his dreams for nearly ten years. He was earning good money, he had a three-year guaranteed contract, he had the beautiful Louise at his side, and most of all, he was doing what he loved.

The Orpheum tour took Hope to some of the premier stages in the United States and Canada. Again, he felt the need for fresh material for jokes. He needed a lot of them and they had to be good. A writer by the name of Al Boasberg had come up with some great gags for the likes of Eddie Cantor, Jack Benny and Burns and Allen. Hope made friends with the man, hoping for some help, perhaps because of his newspaper reviews. They mentioned that frequently his jokes were old and stale. But they liked his style and felt he would be better with new material. Bob paid attention to these reviews and convinced Boasberg to help him out.

Bob's $450 a week allowed him to send the regular $50 a week home to his mother, pay Louise $100 a week, and still have a more than adequate income left over. But now Louise began making demands. The public and the critics were beginning to realize her value in the act and she wanted her own spot. She threatened to quit if Bob didn't come through. She also wanted a more personal commitment from him.

Up against the wall, so to speak, Bob wired home to Mildred and asked her to marry him. It was too late. She had become engaged to someone else. Facing what seemed like the inevitable, Hope asked Louise to marry him. She wasted no time in saying yes, although Hope continued to put off the date.

One of the high points of the prestigious Orpheum tour was Bob's booking at the Cleveland Palace. The visit was special in more ways than one. Not only was Hope showing how far he had come in his career (that 'phase' he was supposed to have been going through), but he was getting his first opportunity to see Avis since his brother Jim had written to him with some disturbing news.

The bulwark of the family, the woman who had kept them together in the worst of times, and who was still there to prove oneself to and to make proud, was thought to have cancer of the cervix. For whatever reason, she refused to go to the doctor and have it treated.

Bob couldn't wait for 'Mahm' to come and see his act. His father, Harry, couldn't come. He wasn't drinking at the time, but was busy working. Avis got so nervous thinking about seeing Bob in all his splendour that she was afraid she would make him nervous if she came. She decided not to attend his opening. Bob was disappointed. Then the next day, after the papers had raved about his performance, she had son Jim take her to the matinee. She was thrilled and so was Bob.

Later in the visit, the brothers sat down and talked a little business. It was just a few weeks after the stock market crash and everybody was beginning to get a little worried – everybody, that is, except Bob. He was confident that vaudeville and the relief it gave people from their cares and woes would thrive.

Bob's brothers, too, were not doing badly. Ivor was in metal products, Fred was in foodstuffs and Jim was doing well with the power company. They put their heads together and decided that buying property would be a good idea. And who better to benefit from it than Avis and Harry?

The brothers looked around and settled on a beautiful house in the exclusive Cleveland Heights section of town. Without telling their parents, the boys bought the house and furnished it completely. Avis was surprised, touched and thrilled.

Soon the tour moved on and another momentous event occurred in Bob Hope's life. Bob Hope is a family man, an entertainer, a humanitarian, a traveller, and last but not least, a golfer. Indeed his latest book, *Confessions of a Hooker*, is devoted to the subject.

In the late 1920s Hope tried the game, but didn't do too well on his first outing and so didn't think about trying again for quite a while. Then, in 1930, on tour with the Diamond brothers from Seattle, he was encouraged to try again, and to his delight found that he played fairly well. From then on he began to play regularly, and now freely admits to being a complete addict.

The tour eventually took Hope to California. Al Boasberg, who was still wiring, writing and calling with new jokes and gags, told Hope he could set up a screen test for him in Hollywood. When the tour reached Los Angeles, Bob called Boasberg's contacts and set a date for the test.

He did part of his regular act before the cameras. It wasn't easy, for there was no audience. After the test, he went on to his next engagement in San Diego and waited to hear from the studio. And waited. And waited. Finally, after a week, he called them when he returned to Los Angeles. He went to a screening room by himself and watched in silence. It was not a happy experience. He thought his nose looked enormous and his whole body seemed funny. As for his performance, it was just downright bad, and it was a relief when it was over.

Bob put the movies and Hollywood out of his mind and headed back on the road with his successful vaudeville tour. He was still aiming to achieve his dream of playing the Palace in New York.

3

'It's De-lovely'

Bob Hope had made his way to Los Angeles via St Paul, Chicago, Cleveland, Winnipeg, Calgary and Vancouver, then south through Seattle, Portland and San Francisco. After his screen test, Bob and Louise completed their first year on the Orpheum Circuit by entertaining audiences in Salt Lake City, Denver, Omaha, Kansas City and St Louis.

To feel better about his screen test, Hope told himself he was too good for Hollywood. He still strongly believed in vaudeville and did not join in with the naysayers who said it was on its last legs. His dream was still to play the Palace. New York, not Tinseltown, would be the Mount Olympus from which he would reign.

When the first year's tour ended, Hope found himself with a couple of months free. Louise went to see her father in Chicago and Bob returned to his family in Cleveland, still riding the white stallion of success.

Bob returned home to his family partly because of word he had received from Avis that George, his youngest brother, seemed to need his help. George, too, had been bitten by the stage bug. Avis thought her elder son could teach and help him.

Bob went back to New York after his visit at home and in the autumn of 1930 again began the Orpheum circuit. He was using Al Boasberg's jokes in a mini-revue called *Antics of 1930*. Louise had a spot, and Bob used his brother, George, as one of two audience stooges. The tour was successful. Audiences loved the act, particularly because it provided relief from the reality of the Depression, which was becoming harder and harder to bear.

Unemployment was doubling. Banks and businesses were closing, and earnings were being reduced. Entertainment, as an escape from life's troubles, was needed more than ever. Radio, movies and vaudeville did well considering other industries' loss of income.

By February of 1931, the act returned again to Cleveland. While there, Hope got some long-awaited good news. At last, he was going to play the Palace!

The next week saw Bob alternating between fits of total panic, moods of euphoric happiness and serious thoughts about how to make his act better. Hope's *Antics of 1931* was to play opposite Gershwin's *Of Thee I Sing*, the first musical comedy to win a Pulitzer Prize; Fred and Adele Astaire in *The Band Wagon*; Al Jolson in *The Wonder Bar*; and Gertrude Lawrence and Noel Coward in Coward's *Private Lives*.

Bob sensed the need for a gimmick to set his own act apart from the others in order to get people talking and fill the seats of the Palace. The gimmick he chose was a staged mock picket-line outside the theatre, with his stooges carrying comical signs stating that Hope was unfair to them. Crowds did gather, and most of the New York papers carried an account of the event. It was a gamble, but it paid off in larger audiences.

Despite the substantial audiences, Hope's act was not a big success. Few critics chose to review his performances and the reviews that did appear were lukewarm to downright hostile.

This poor reception only mildly dampened Bob's enthusiasm, however. He felt that he hadn't been giving his best performances, and he knew he could do better. At least it wouldn't hurt to have the New York Palace on his *curriculum vitae*, and the experience would serve him in good stead.

As 1932 began, the United States was entering probably the worst year of the Depression. By that summer, 13 million Americans were unemployed; wages were 60 per cent below those of 1929; industry was operating at half the capacity of 1929; $6 billion in business losses were registered; agriculture prices were still falling; and banks continued to close. The situation was even worse in parts of Europe. Germany's Weimar Republic devalued the Deutschmark so much that huge sums of money were required just to buy a loaf of bread.

Bob Hope, however, continued to prosper financially. At this time he was making around $1,000 a week. In fact, many actors and entertainers were doing very well as the public demand for escapism remained strong. Hope's regular income allowed him to take on some of the more visible trappings of success, specifically a new Packard and chauffeur to go with it.

With constant work, Hope's delivery of his material became steadily better. His timing had always been excellent, and now he was perfecting his ability to take others' writing and make it seem fresh and spontaneous. He had found new writers since Al Boasberg had gone on to Hollywood.

Hope had come to the attention of Broadway producers and was asked to be in a show called *Ballyhoo*. It wasn't the most terrific show to hit the boards, and it lasted only 16 weeks. However, in a number of ways it was momentous for Bob's future.

The *Ballyhoo* offer had not included Louise, and resulted in their breakup. They had actually taken out a marriage licence in January, 1932, but never acted on it. By the time rehearsals started for the Broadway show that summer, they had separated.

During the run of *Ballyhoo*, Hope and two others were asked to join in an experiment. They appeared on the New York CBS television station W2XAB. The technical quality of the broadcast was so bad that everyone involved agreed that the new medium would never make it.

Hope's greatest public exposure, perhaps, came from radio. At this time he made his first appearance on Rudy Vallee's show, to which 23 million people regularly listened.

Hope also started doing benefits. They were as good for him as he was for them. They gave him an opportunity to work out new material and work with a lot of important people, and they did wonderful things for his public image. And of course, he was still Avis' son, so he believed that this was the right thing to do.

In October, 1932, while *Ballyhoo* was still running, Hope bumped into a man at the Friar's Club with whom he swapped a few stories. This was Harry Lillis 'Bing' Crosby, an actor/singer who was riding high. His first big movie, *The Big Broadcast of 1932*, had just been released with great success and his new solo singing record was a top-seller. Crosby was a star.

When *Ballyhoo* closed, Bob was ready. He had seen the handwriting on the wall, and had got himself booked into the Capitol Theatre in New York a couple of days later, 2 December 1932. To

Bob's surprise and delight, he would be sharing the bill with the crooner, the famous Bing Crosby. Hope had liked him when they met before and had felt they could work well together. The feeling was mutual. The two entertainers soon became friends.

Together the pair worked out a routine. They hadn't planned to work together at all, but Bing suggested it and Hope readily agreed. It was obvious that they thought each other funny, and they had such a good time on stage that audiences loved them. Right from the beginning, they would take turns as to who played straight and who played the clown. Their affectionate insults and rapid delivery were very effective and remained a trademark of their work together until Crosby passed away several years ago.

As 1932 drew to a close, Bob was increasingly disturbed by the news from home. Avis' health continued to get worse. She was now bedridden, and the doctors gave her no more than a year to live. They told her family that she might have even less time. Bob had a telephone installed at her bedside, and phoned and wrote often.

After the Capitol Theatre engagement, Bob returned to the Palace again. The Palace had begun to lose its lustre and was unable to fill its seats as in its heyday. Good could still come from appearing in this fabled old house, though. Bob's act was spotted by a producer who wanted him for his new Broadway play, a musical comedy.

The play was called *Roberta* and it was a big boost for Bob Hope's career. Bob's life was definitely looking up, he had a new agent, Louis Shurr, and if it weren't for the constant concern about his mother, his life would be worry-free.

The cast of *Roberta* included some very famous and soon-to-be famous names. There was George Murphy, who started as a chorus boy and would go on to become a United States Senator after a successful career in the movies. (Acting has led to politics more than once in America. At the time of this writing, Clint Eastwood is running for the office of Mayor of Carmel, California!) Murphy was to become a lifelong friend of Hope's. In other small parts were Sydney Greenstreet, Fred MacMurray, and Imogene Coca. The score was by Jerome Kern and included the now-classic song, 'Smoke Gets in Your Eyes'.

Roberta didn't take New York by storm when it first opened. However, although critics didn't much care for it, audiences kept coming and it became the second most successful show of the winter of 1933–34.

On a cold night in December 1933, Hope's new pal, George Murphy, decided that Bob needed some cheering up. He knew Avis' health worried Bob greatly. He and Louise had called it quits and there hadn't been anyone to replace her. George talked Bob into coming along with some others after the show for a drink at the Vogue Club. (Prohibition had recently been repealed.) The singer at the club was Dolores Reade, a tall, beautiful, graceful woman with a lovely singing voice. She was singing 'It's Only a Paper Moon' when Hope and his companions walked into the club. After her performance, she joined the group at their table, having dated one of the men from time to time. That man soon bowed out and Bob and Dolores began talking. They kept it up through another act they went to see, as well as through a late deli supper. Bob liked her a lot. He invited her to see *Roberta* and gave her tickets for the matinee on Wednesday, 27 December.

Bob went home to Cleveland for Christmas to see his mother. He found himself talking and thinking about Dolores most of the time. After the Wednesday matinee, Bob waited backstage impatiently for her to come back and talk to him. She didn't show up, and he was terribly disappointed.

Dolores had gone to the matinee as planned, but was shocked to find that Bob was not in the chorus. Discovering that he had a starring role, she was too embarrassed to go backstage. After all, the day after their first meeting she had told her mother that she had met the man she was going to marry, and here he was, a Broadway star!

Bob finally found the courage to return to the Vogue Club and see her. After she explained what had happened, they were back on track. Dolores still lived with her mother, who looked upon Bob almost as blackly as Mildred's mother had done. As an Irish Catholic she intended to have her daughters marry Irish Catholics and wasn't thrilled with Bob Hope as a prospective son-in-law.

In mid-January, Dolores got an engagement in Miami. She and Bob heated up the telephone lines between Florida and New York confessing their love for each other. Absence was definitely making hearts grow fonder.

On Sunday, 22 January 1934, sad news came from Cleveland. Avis Townes Hope, the proud mother of seven sons and beloved of them all, had passed away. In a way, it was a relief for everyone that she had died. She had been in constant pain, and had long been wasting away, so death had at least put an end to her suffering.

Bob went home for the funeral. When he returned to New York, he knew how much he really needed Dolores. Dolores gave the Miami nightclub notice and soon took a train north. The two met in Erie, Pennsylvania, a city they chose for unknown reasons, and were married on 19 February 1934. He was 30 years old and she was 29.

They had little time for honeymooning. Within two days, Bob was back on stage, as well as continuing regular radio spots. All in all, he was making a tidy sum of money. Both he and Dolores felt secure and happy.

Bob's agent, Louis Shurr, got him another screen test, this time in New York. Shurr was pushing many of his clients toward the movies. Both Fred MacMurry and George Murphy had gone from *Roberta* to Hollywood, although Bob didn't seem ready for California.

The new screen test was better than his first one, but Bob's negative attitude toward Tinseltown was intensified by Dolores' criticism of his second screen test. She thought he looked like a turtle on the screen. However, he did take a contract to make six short features in Astoria, Queens, New York. The money was good, and Bob could work in Queens during the day and still appear on stage at night.

Hope left *Roberta* in June and set up an East Coast vaudeville tour for the summer. He and Dolores worked together on stage and toured for ten weeks. She sang and he cut up. He had a couple of new writers and had improved his material. Both critics and audiences loved it.

Word of their success made its way back to Broadway, with a little help from Louis Shurr, and Hope was signed for a play called *Say When*. The show turned out to be a huge success with the critics, but unfortunately there were production problems and it closed very early. Hope's star status was secure, however. Shortly after the musical closed, he began doing a new regular radio show for Bromo-Seltzer, called the *Intimate Revue*.

The *Intimate Revue* saw the first appearance in Hope's act of a character called 'Honey Chile', a dumb blonde with a Southern accent who played comic bits with him. There were several Honey Chiles over the years, and the concept worked for a long time.

Hope and Honey Chile did well in the *Intimate Revue*. The critics had good things to say and the fans sent in bags of mail. However, the praise came too late to improve the listener ratings enough to satisfy the sponsors and the show was cancelled on 5 April 1935.

That spring, Hope went on the road again with Dolores and Honey Chile. From time to time, he would return to New York to shoot the short feature movies he had promised to do. The work was hard, the hours were long (especially for Hope, who had become a night owl), but the money was very good.

He was cast in the new Ziegfeld Follies late that summer, although the show, which was to open in Boston, would not start until Christmastime. The cast was outstanding. It included Josephine Baker, Eve Arden, Edgar Bergen and Charlie McCarthy, as well as the famous Fanny Brice. Vincente Minelli designed the production, Ira Gershwin wrote the lyrics, Ogden Nash and Billy Rose contributed material and George Ballanchine did the choreography. During the rehearsals, Bob also signed to appear as the comedy star of the *Atlantic White Flash* radio programme.

During the run of the Ziegfeld Follies of 1936, the beloved Fanny Brice was frequently indisposed. She suffered a great deal of arthritis and had teeth problems for which she took medication. Nonetheless, she was on hand in May of that year to celebrate the thirty-fifth anniversary of the Shubert theatrical dynasty. Since the death of Flo Ziegfeld, the Shuberts had been working with his widow to produce the Follies. The anniversary celebration brought together some of the greatest performers of all time: Al Jolson, Lou Holtz, Sophie Tucker, Jack Benny, Bert Lahr, Ethel Barrymore, Helen Hayes, Kit Cornell, and of course Fanny Brice. Bob Hope was the MC.

Sadly, a week after this gala, the Ziegfeld Follies was forced to close down due to Brice's poor health. Bob worked that summer on his radio show, completed his commitment for the short films and performed numerous benefits.

Bob Hope's lifestyle remains practically unchanged from those early days. He and Dolores are very close. Bob is a late riser, but once up, it's rare for him to take a break in his activity. Their home is a comfortable refuge. Golf is played as often as possible. Dolores remains a devout Catholic, contributing a great deal of her time to Church charities and activities, and the two throw wonderful parties with highly coveted invitations.

During the summer of 1936, plans were underway to mount a new Broadway musical extravaganza that would celebrate the gaiety returning to the American spirit following the Depression. The show was absolutely stellar. It was called *Red, Hot and Blue!* and was written by Cole Porter. Hope shared top billing with the great Ethel Merman and the 'Schnozzola', Jimmy Durante. Also included was Vivian Vance, who later played Lucille Ball's sidekick for many years on television.

The plot to this musical comedy was inconsequential and no more than a vehicle to showcase the antics of the stars and the show's beautiful Cole Porter music. One of the highlights was a duet by Merman and Hope of 'It's De-Lovely'. Merman also sang 'Down in the Depths on the 90th Floor'.

Giant egos shaped the success of *Red, Hot and Blue!* Durante would fracture the words of the script, Merman would bring down the roof with her voice and Hope would ad lib at the slightest opportunity. Of course each star laboured to ensure that the others didn't steal the show, and in the process gave the audience outstanding performances, fresh and exciting each time.

Hope continued with his benefits, frequently being cited as the most generous with his time of all the stars then on Broadway. He couldn't outdo Durante, though, and frequently the two 'noses' could be seen working together to raise money for one cause or another. Despite playing numerous practical jokes on each other, the two remained good friends, and the relationship was to last for the rest of Durante's life.

Thanks to frequent jibes on their respective radio shows, the Crosby–Hope rivalry gag was becoming well known. Cole Porter entered into the spirit of the thing in one of the songs he wrote for Merman:

> Oh, charming sir, the way you sing
> Would break the heart of Missus Crosby's Bing
> For the tone of your tra la la
> Has that certain je ne sais quoi.

Bob recorded his first phonograph record from this show: it was 'It's De-Lovely', playing at 78 rpm. On the flip side Ethel Merman sang 'Down in the Depths'.

After New York, *Red, Hot and Blue!* moved on to Chicago where it closed quickly on 3 May 1937, after a two-week run. Its stars were prepared.

Ethel Merman went off to make a movie called *Happy Landing* with Sonja Henie and Don Ameche. Jimmy Durante carried on with nightclubs and vaudeville acts. Bob Hope returned to New York to prepare for an audition as the host of a Jergens-Woodbury Soap radio show called *Rippling Rhythm Revue*, which was to air on NBC. Bob was hired, and used a combination of monologue and banter with Honey Chile (now played by the third young lady to hold the job).

Radio was influenced by corporate business more than Hope's stage work had been. Programmes had sponsors whose goal was to sell their products. Hope, convinced that radio was a good medium for him and one in which he could be increasingly successful, felt that he needed some help in understanding the business side of it.

Fortunately, he met a man named Jimmy Saphier who was an expert in the field. The two men got along very well together, and Saphier became Hope's agent. Both signed a contract for one year. Their agreement was never renewed and a new one never written. It wasn't needed. The men continued to work together for almost the next 40 years until Saphier died in 1974.

Hope had also learned about the importance of public relations and publicity. He felt his charitable work should be publicized to keep his name before the public eye, and he wanted to be sure that what was said was favourable. He began looking for a good publicity agent.

A few weeks into the Woodbury radio show, Bob finally received a Hollywood offer that, unlike previous offers, was one that he couldn't refuse. Paramount signed him for the film *The Big Broadcast of 1938* in June, 1937. Before he left, he had a few things to take care of.

Hope soon found the publicity agent he wanted. Mack Millar knew all the influential columnists and critics, was well respected, and did a great job for his clients. However, there was one obstacle. Bob and Dolores were going to California, and it seemed unlikely that Millar would want to leave New York, even though he had almost as many connections on the West Coast as the East.

Bob went to talk to Millar. To his delight, he learned that another one of Millar's big clients was making the move west, and Millar had decided to go as well. The publicity agent actually started working for Hope while he was still in New York, setting up some important and favourable interviews for him.

Bob's next problem was the radio show. Bob wanted to continue it, which meant that he needed to convince the producers to move the show to Los Angeles. Here Jimmy Saphier proved his value, negotiating with Woodbury and NBC so that Bob could continue the show from Hollywood.

There was one sad note in Bob's life that spring. Harry Hope had never really recovered from losing his dear Avis. He passed away at the age of 66.

The Hope–Crosby gags were becoming more important. Each man had his own radio show and the pair would trade barbs over the air. Some of the names they came up with for each other stuck and were used throughout their long relationship. Crosby's names for Hope had to do with his looks and his age. He called him 'Shovel Head', 'Scoop Nose', 'Ski Nose', or often just plain 'Dad'. Hope retaliated with references to Crosby's problems maintaining his weight. Some of his favourite names were 'Mattress Hip', 'Blubber', and 'Lard'.

Dolores began packing at the apartment on Central Park West. The Hopes were going to the Land of Sunshine in California. Bob's career began to rise so steadily that today, now that he is so well known and loved, he is truly in a class by himself.

4

Your Hollywood Parade

By September, everything was finally ready. Bob and Dolores boarded the Super Chief and headed West. They arrived in Pasedena on 9 September 1937 and checked into the Beverly-Wilshire Hotel. Bob would be starting his first real feature film almost immediately.

Hollywood at that time was a very special place. Although already recognized as *the* seat of American movie-making, it was still a very young and new town. There were glitz and glamour, deals and movie moguls, fantasy and illusion. The stars seemed larger than life to their fans, who crowded the town hoping for a glimpse of the glamorous figures who graced the big screen. And there were always the ever-hopefuls who wanted to join the club – the starlets, the actors who rehearsed by night and parked cars by day, the would-be writers, directors, producers, animators – in short, everyone touched by the fantastical world of the silver screen.

In 1937, Hollywood was dominated by the studios and the men who ran them. Just ten years before, Al Jolson had made *The Jazz Singer*, the first feature-length film to use passages of dialogue, and 'talkies' were born. By 1929, silents were virtually dead. The coming of sound brought several changes to the industry.

Sound movies were more expensive to make than silents had been. This fact drove a number of the smaller production companies out of business, consolidating the power of the major studios. Sound also ended many Hollywood careers as some silent film stars were found to have poor voices. The call went out to Broadway and the legitimate stage for actors and actresses with trained voices. Stage actors, who had hitherto scorned this new industry, were now arriving in droves.

Another positive effect of sound was the enthusiastic response of the movie-going public. In 1927, about 57 million movie tickets per week were sold. That number almost doubled by 1930. Wall Street investors took notice and money began pouring into Hollywood. Five major studios made it to the top of the heap and would dominate the town for many years. These were Paramount, Fox (later 20th Century Fox), MGM, Warner Brothers and RKO. After the 'Big Five', there were the 'Little Three', Columbia, Universal and United Artists.

During the Depression, the studios had some financial problems, but managed to weather them. Each 'dream factory' developed its own stable of directors, writers and stars whom it ruled with an iron fist. Each one also developed its own characteristic style of films.

MGM (Metro-Goldwyn-Mayer) was a subsidiary of the wealthiest company in film, Loew's, which owned the greatest number of movie theatres around the country. With its enormous financial resources, MGM boasted that it possessed 'More Stars Than There Are in Heaven'. The studio lavished money on its productions under the overall leadership of Louis B. Mayer and Irving Thalberg.

By 1937, MGM's most successful productions included *Anna Christie* (Greta Garbo's first talkie); *Dinner at Eight* with Marie Dressler, Wallace Beery, Jean Harlow and Lionel Barrymore; *Camille; The Thin Man; The Champ*; and the Marx Brothers' *A Night at the Opera*.

Paramount was MGM's closest rival. Paramount's pictures had less uniformity than those at MGM, while the directors seemed to have more personal creative control. Paramount had under contract such famous directors as Cecil B. DeMille and Ernst Lubitsch. Its stable of stars included Marlene Dietrich, Gary Cooper, Claudette Colbert, Fredric March and George Raft. Some of Paramount's better known films prior to 1937 included *The Plainsman, Cleopatra, Trouble in Paradise, The Scarlet Empress*, and *The Devil Is a Woman* (the last two starring Paramount's answer to MGM's Garbo, Marlene Dietrich).

Warner Brothers was very different from either MGM or Paramount. The Warner brothers ran their studio very tightly, insisting on both strict discipline and penny-pinching cost controls. The Warners kept their actors and directors working constantly and at a breakneck pace. This prompted frequent legal battles with their talent, especially the strong-minded Bette Davis. Miss Davis struggled hard to avoid the mediocre roles Warner's kept wanting her to take. Bad as the films often were, her performances were so strong that audiences and critics loved her. She won her first Oscar in 1935 for *Dangerous*. She also managed to get a good role in *The Petrified Forest*, but her next two movies were dreadful. In rebellion, she refused the next role the studio asked her to play. Warner Brothers got a court injunction for violation of contract, and Miss Davis promptly sued. Although she lost the case, Warner's ironically began to show her more respect and give her more suitable roles.

The Warners' strong control and breakneck production schedules gave a sameness to the plots and the look of their studio's films. They tended to concentrate on gangsters and social concerns, reflecting the Depression and its headlines. In 1931, Warner's released *Little Caesar* with Edward G. Robinson, followed shortly by James Cagney in *Public Enemy*. Warner's also produced prison melodramas with themes of social justice, notably *I Am a Fugitive From a Chain Gang*. Melodrama also showed up in Warner's romances, such as the swashbuckling *Captain Blood* and *The Charge of the Light Brigade*, both starring Errol Flynn and Olivia de Havilland.

Universal studios focused on horror and fantasy films. These low-budget films have endured as some of the best classics ever produced. Some of the more famous include *Dracula* with Bela Lugosi and *Frankenstein* with Boris Karloff. These two stars, joined by Lon Chaney, made up Hollywood's horror gallery. Universal frightened everyone with *The Mummy, The Invisible Man, The Bride of Frankenstein, The Werewolf of London* and *The Wolf Man*. Occasionally, Universal produced more spectacular, expensive films like the classics *All Quiet on the Western Front* and *Showboat*.

The Fox studio had the pleasure of holding under contract the nation's biggest box office draw: Shirley Temple. Born in 1928, Shirley began appearing in movies before she was four years old. At the end of her first year with Fox, she won a special Academy Award 'in grateful recognition of her outstanding contribution to screen entertainment during the year 1934'. By 1938, she was Hollywood's biggest box office attraction.

RKO was smaller and less consistent than many of the other

Bob Hope

studios, although it did manage to turn out some all-time favourite films featuring some of the greatest stars ever to grace the silver screen. There was Fae Wray in *King Kong; Of Human Bondage* with Bette Davis (on loan from Warners'); *Little Women* with Katharine Hepburn; and *Sylvia Scarlett*, with Hepburn playing opposite Cary Grant in one of his earliest films.

Columbia studios was run by the legendary Harry Cohn, an autocratic, dictatorial, obnoxious but thoroughly brilliant man. Cohn was ruthless and vulgar as well as probably the most feared and hated man in Hollywood. However, no one could argue with his successs. He made Columbia successful and profitable and turned a number of actors and actresses into stars, notably Rita Hayworth. Frank Capra worked for Cohn and continually directed hits for the studio, including *It Happened One Night, Mr. Deeds Goes to Town* and *Lost Horizon*. Columbia put little of its talent under contract, preferring to borrow from other studios. Some of the gems that resulted from this practice included *Holiday* with Kate Hepburn and Cary Grant and Howard Hawks' *The Awful Truth*, also with Grant, who had left the studio contract system early.

By the time Bob Hope arrived in Hollywood, the movie business had recovered from the Depression and was about to enter one of its most prolific periods. The studios not only produced movies, but owned the theatres those movies ran in. Every level of production was controlled by the studios, from technicians to creative personnel.

The Hays Office had put its regulatory Production Code into strict effect in 1934. This was the code of 'good taste' designed to keep scandal and bad reputations out of the public mind. This code, along with the strong studio system, tended to provide a kind of consistency to movies of the era and created a fantasy world of perfect people who neither swore nor had sex. Violence was allowed, though, as long as it wasn't too gruesome.

Bob's first feature film was *The Big Broadcast of 1938* for Paramount. His co-stars were W. C. Fields, Martha Raye, Dorothy Lamour and Shirley Ross. He found it a pleasure to work with Dorothy Lamour, an old friend from New York. A modern reviewer calls this movie a 'hodgepodge of bad musical numbers . . . notable only for Fields' few scenes [and] Hope and Ross' song

"Thanks for the Memory"'. Bob knew he liked the song from the moment he first heard it at the studio.

Hope had three problems in the making of this first movie. First, the studio wanted him to have his nose fixed. Fortunately, Dolores violently objected and his 'ski-nose' was kept intact.

Secondly, Bob had to learn how to turn his vaudeville delivery into something that would work well on camera. Since there was no audience, he couldn't take his usual pause after delivering a funny line. It was a hard habit to break, but he managed. He also realized how close the camera got, closer even than the people in the front row. He had to learn to use his eyes. Under a good director, he learned well.

The last problem was publicity. *The Big Broadcast* was made at Paramount, and the Paramount stable of stars provided some tough competition for the newcomer. Burns and Allen, Jack Benny, Harold Lloyd, Martha Raye, Charlie Ruggles and the amazing Mae West were all comedians under contract. The Paramount publicity department did good work, but Hope wanted to be sure he didn't get lost in the shuffle. He felt he should get the most out of every 'news' item. Mack Millar helped him out.

The big news about Hope was that in November, Paramount liked the rushes from *The Big Broadcast* well enough to pick up their option on Bob's initial contract and sign him for seven years. His contract called for three pictures per year at a starting fee of $20,000 per film. Paramount reserved the right to cancel its option at any time.

Hope was next cast in *College Swing. College Swing* turned out to be a low-budget, forgettable film. Bob got fourth billing, after Martha Raye and before Betty Grable.

Along with movie-making, Hope finished his commitment to the Woodbury radio show. He also renewed contact with old friends in Hollywood and met new ones who would be important through the rest of his career. His new friends included Skinnay Ennis, a singer, and Jerry Colonna, a trombone player. These two became featured performers in his acts on the road and radio for many, many years, particularly the later military tours.

Hope also got the chance to deepen his friendship with Bing Crosby. Crosby was truly one of Paramount's brightest stars and biggest box office attractions. The studio lavished publicity on him, and occasionally Hope profited from it as well. Early on, Paramount staged a golf tournament for the two, partnering

Crosby with the famous columnist, Ed Sullivan. Hope lost, and as his penalty spent a day as an extra on Crosby's latest film.

Hope decided that radio was a good way to keep his name on the public's lips. He pestered Jimmy Saphier to get him a new programme, and he continued to do benefits almost as often as he was asked. Finally, Saphier got him a guest spot on *Your Hollywood Parade*. The show was sponsored by Lucky Strike. Bob did well enough to be offered a regular feature spot, and stayed with the show until it closed in March, 1938.

By then, *The Big Broadcast* had premiered and Hope was a hit. The critics singled him out for stardom and the song 'Thanks for the Memory' went on to earn its composers an Oscar.

The pace of Bob's life grew hectic while he was making his third film, *Give me a Sailor*, again with Martha Raye and Betty Grable. Between the benefits, the publicity appearances and the shooting schedule, Bob needed some help in organizing his time. He thought of his brother Jack back in Ohio. Jack quickly agreed to help 'old Les' and came out to California.

After his third movie, Hope took to the stage again while Jimmy Saphier tried to nail down a new radio contract. They were also waiting for Paramount to come up with another picture. In the interim, Bob recreated his role in *Roberta* for a Los Angeles run. Following that, he and Dolores went on the road with Jackie Coogan.* They performed on the Loew's vaudeville circuit while Paramount, which had delayed putting him back on screen, now had to wait for Bob to begin work on a new film they had for him. This was *Thanks for the Memory*, again with Shirley Ross.

When the Hopes returned to Los Angeles in July, they moved

---

* Coogan had been a child star, first working with Charlie Chaplin, and then in a series of very highly paid roles. As so often happens with child stars, his career took a nose dive as he grew up. In 1935, when he turned 21, he was due to be paid the $4 million he had earned as a child. That same year, his father was killed in a car accident. His mother and new stepfather attempted to keep Jackie's money. Coogan, then married to Betty Grable, filed suit. By the time the suit was settled, his money had dwindled to just a quarter of a million dollars of which Jackie got half. The case led to the passage of the California Child Actors Bill, known as the Coogan Act. In 1939, he and Grable divorced over money matters. Today, he is perhaps best known for his television role as Uncle Festus in *The Addams Family*.

into a home in the Toluca Lake section of North Hollywood. Earlier, Bob had bought three acres of land for $6,000 and quickly built a house on it. (A few years later, an adjoining three-acre plot cost him ten times that amount.) The house was a convenient walk from Warner Brothers, Universal and Columbia. Some of the Hopes' neighbours included Bing Crosby, W. C. Fields, Mary Astor, Ruby Keeler, Jimmy Cagney, Humphrey Bogart, and the Nelsons (Ozzie and Harriet). Perhaps the most attractive feature of the site was its closeness to the Lakeside Golf Course.

Dolores liked the feeling of permanence, and enthusiastically went about the job of making their house a home. She and Bob both wanted children, but it was becoming obvious that the only way to get them would be through adoption.

Saphier at last finished negotiations for a new radio show, of which Bob was not only the star but the producer. The sponsor was Pepsodent. Again, Bob looked for something to make his show stand out from the others. His biggest competition would be Jack Benny and Edgar Bergen and Charlie McCarthy, the ventriloquist and his dummy who managed to enchant audiences that could not see their act, only hear it.

To ensure a continuing supply of fresh material, Bob hired what became known as 'Hope's Army', a crew of ten or eleven young, competitive (and inexpensive) writers who could turn out enough gags and sketches to fill a half-hour every week. Skinnay Ennis and Jerry Colonna were added as weekly attractions along with a singing group called Six Hits and a Miss.

The guest star for the first show was the lovely actress Constance Bennett. (One of the string of sophisticated comedies in which she had starred was *Topper* in 1937 with Cary Grant.) Later guest stars that first season included George Burns, Groucho Marx, and of course, Bing Crosby. Hope and Crosby would trade guest spots, each appearance adding fuel to the fire of their 'feud'. They constantly tried to trip each other up with comic ad libs.

Hope began to use 'Thanks for the Memory' as his theme song for the radio show. It became his lifelong signature song, its lyrics rewritten to fit each occasion.

The show's premiere in October, 1938, was a hit. *Variety* said on 5 October 1938:

That small speck going over the centre field fence is the four-bagger Bob Hope whammed out his first time at bat for Pepsodent. If he can keep up the pace he'll get as much word of mouth for 1938–1939 as Edgar Bergen got for 1937–1938. He sounded like success all the way. Hope must be trying because the script showed plenty of thought. But it's his particular gift not to seem to be trying. And that's a great psychological aid. It suggests wearing qualities.

Or, maybe, we're neglecting the writers. Whoever he or them is/are, house rules allow an extra bow.

In the meantime, Bob and Dolores looked into the possibility of becoming adoptive parents. Their good friends George Burns and Gracie Allen recommended The Cradle, an orphanage in Evanston, Illinois. It had one of the best reputations in the country. The Hopes began the adoption process, sadly realizing, however, that it could take a long time for their dreams to come true.

Soon two more films were ready for Bob to shoot, a 'B' movie called *Never Say Die* with Martha Raye, and *Some Like it Hot* (later retitled *Rhythm Romance*) with Shirley Ross. Neither was a big hit.

Between the benefits and the radio show, Hope was earning a reputation as *the* MC in Hollywood. Therefore, it was logical for him to be asked to be a presenter at the 1939 Academy Awards presentation. It was his first of many appearances at that annual event.

Bob's growing reputation on radio and his wide popularity finally convinced Paramount to put him in a better picture. The movie they chose was *The Cat and the Canary* and Bob's co-star was Paulette Goddard. Goddard, who had been a Ziegfeld girl at the young age of 14, emigrated to Hollywood in 1931. Not long after, she met Charlie Chaplin and eventually married him. They made the classic film *Modern Times* together in 1936.

The Cat and the Canary is often credited with giving Hope his first real claim to movie stardom. The movie was a spoof of the horror melodramas of the day, complete with an old dark house. Bob's role was tailor-made for him, and his performance was praised by critics and fans alike.

Hope's success had been predicted by none other than Charlie

Chaplin. Chaplin came by the set to see Paulette and stayed to see some of the rushes. The 'Little Tramp' turned to an astonished and pleased Hope and said, 'You are one of the best timers of comedy I have ever seen.'

In March of 1939, Hope received a letter from his Aunt Lucy back in England. She lived with Grandfather James, now 96. The family had heard that Harry's son had made good in America and she wanted to hear all about it. It caused him to do something extraordinary: Bob Hope actually planned a vacation.

As might be expected, Bob made plans to work his act into his vacation schedule. Filming on *The Cat and the Canary* would take him through the month of May. The last Pepsodent show of the season would be 20 June, and people wanted Bob to do some vaudeville that summer. He and Dolores decided that they would make their way to New York via the vaudeville dates. From there, they would take a steamer to England and meet the relatives, then go on to Paris, a place Dolores had always wanted to visit.

More thrilling to Dolores than even the chance to see Paris was the fact that the tour would take them to Chicago. The Cradle was in Evanston, Illinois, practically a suburb of the Windy City.

The Hopes had passed their preliminary interviews as adoptive parents, and while the more detailed examinations of their characters proceeded, they performed vaudeville. When they finally got to Evanston, they faced tough interviews, focusing on the problems that the children of celebrities could have. The Hopes seemed to pass muster, though, and felt encouraged that they might have a child waiting for them when they returned from Europe.

On the way to New York, they stopped and met with their Pepsodent sponsor. The man slipped Bob an envelope as they were leaving, saying he had heard that they were on their way to Europe and wanted to offer something that might come in handy. That evening, Bob opened the envelope. It contained round-trip, de luxe suite tickets for the ship and a letter of credit for $2,500.

In Cleveland, there was a minor family reunion of the Hope brothers. Fred, Sid, Ivor, Jack and Bob were all there with their wives. George was working in Hollywood at the writing job he'd found through Bob. Jim was rumoured to be on the West Coast. He had been trying show business himself, but was not doing particularly well; the others felt he was envious of Bob. Ivor and

Bob talked business. They were going to be partners in Hope Metal Products, with Ivor running the company.

Bob finished up the vaudeville tour in New York, then had a special day as Mayor LaGuardia declared 'Bob Hope Day at the Fair'. 'The Fair,' of course, was the 1939 World's Fair.

Soon it was time to board the *Normandie*. The docks were packed with enthusiastic fans and autograph seekers, seeing off a list of celebrity passengers. On the same crossing were Mr and Mrs Charles Boyer, Norma Shearer, George Raft and Edward G. Robinson as well as other well-known entertainers. Also on board were a best-selling author, the Irish prime minister, and Eleanor Roosevelt, who was there to see her uncle David Gray and Treasury Secretary Henry Morgenthau off on the voyage.

The press gathered round everyone including Bob. They asked him for details of the family reunion. They even asked his opinion on the worsening political situation in Europe. Hitler was causing concern on several fronts and people who feared the Nazi regime had already begun emigrating. Bob said, 'There won't be a war.' To Hope and many others it seemed difficult to imagine that a war could develop amid the post-Depression mood of prosperity and gaiety.

The Hopes thoroughly enjoyed England. In London Bob and Dolores went to the theatre, played golf, visited Bob's birthplace in Eltham and generally relaxed. In the second week of their visit, they went to Hitchin to see Grandfather James, the 96-year-old patriarch of the Hope family. Still spry and mentally sharp, he helped a faltering Bob tell a few jokes to the family when Bob's American delivery proved difficult for this new English audience to follow.

After the visit, Bob and Dolores finally left to see Paris, long a dream of Dolores'. Unfortunately, their timing was not good. War was approaching fast. After an evening of transatlantic phone calls, the Hopes decided to return home as soon as they could. Louella Parsons, who had been predicting a conflict, wrote the following lead item in her column for 25 August 1939:

> With war imminent, Hollywood yesterday realized how many of its important stars are still in Europe. Tyrone Power . . . Charles Boyer . . . Robert Montgomery . . . Maureen O'Sullivan . . . Bob Hope, who planned a European holiday, is cutting his visit short to hurry home.

Bob and Dolores had tickets on the *Queen Mary* for the middle of September. Few suspected that her 30 August sailing would be the last civilian crossing she would make until after the war. The Hopes joined hundreds of other frightened people from both America and Europe to cross the Channel and make their way to the ship in Southampton. They managed to get a first class suite on the terribly overcrowded ship.

While they were at sea the dread news came on 3 September 1939. England and France had declared war on Germany. Hitler's troops were destroying Polish villages and towns. Rumours were rife on the *Queen Mary* that the Germans were sending submarines to sink the ship. The passengers received black-out instructions.

Hope was scheduled to do a show that night in the salon. He didn't think it would be appropriate, but the captain told him that comedy was probably the best medicine for the nervous passengers. In the best theatrical tradition, Bob agreed to go on with the show.

Bob got on stage and performed his regular routine for about an hour. His closing, though, was very special; he had written new lyrics for his theme song for the occasion:

> Thanks for the memory
> Of this great ocean trip
> On England's finest ship.
> Tho' they packed them to the rafters
> They never made a slip.
> Ah! Thank you so much.
>
> Thanks for the memory
> Some folks slept on the floor,
> Some in the corridor;
> But I was more exclusive,
> My room had 'Gentlemen' above the door,
> Ah! Thank you so much.

It was just what the doctor ordered. The audience adored it. The Captain asked for a copy for the ship's log and copies were distributed to the passengers. When the ship reached New York, Mack Millar, in true publicity agent form, sent a copy to *Variety*,

which printed it with its catalogue of celebrities returning from
Europe.

Safe back home in America, the Hopes went directly to The
Cradle in Evanston. Good news was waiting for them; they had
passed the final inspection and had been approved as adoptive
parents. The only hitch was that they had requested a boy, and
the agency had an eight-week-old girl for them. Sensing that Bob
was disappointed, the director decided to make the Hopes wait
to be sure they would be really committed parents.

The Hopes returned to California. A week later, the phone
rang. The legal papers had cleared, and they could come and pick
up their daughter. Dolores went by herself and brought back
Linda Theresa. Bob, the family man, now had a family of his own.
He called his daughter little Puzzle-Head.

5

'There is a Man'

When she was 13 years old, Judy Garland (born Frances Gumm) was auditioned personally by Louis B. Mayer, the production chief at MGM. He was so impressed with her voice that he immediately signed her to a contract without even giving her a screen test. By then, of course, she had already been performing for ten years in a vaudeville act.

Broadway Melody of 1938 was only her third appearance on screen, but Judy Garland stole the show from the likes of Eleanor Powell and Sophie Tucker. The highlight of the film was Judy singing 'Dear Mr. Gable' to a photograph of Clark Gable. She was soon cast opposite Mickey Rooney, and began the first of nine movies she would make with the young star.

The picture which made her a world-class star was *The Wizard of Oz*, released in 1939. The power and emotion that the young girl put into the song 'Over the Rainbow' instantly endeared her to millions. Judy went on to win a special Oscar as 'The Best Juvenile Performer of the Year' for her role as Dorothy. Ironically, the role originally had been intended for Shirley Temple.

In the first season of the Pepsodent radio show, Judy had been a guest of Hope's. Now, at the beginning of the 1939–1940 season, she was signed on as a regular. She stayed with the show for two years, bantering with Hope and singing out to America in her beautiful voice.

That autumn was a great time for Bob Hope. The 'Pepsodent Show' had earned the third-highest ratings in the country, and now his latest film, *The Cat and the Canary*, opened to spectacular reviews.

Paramount had a new script it wished to develop called *The Road to Singapore*, the tale of a pair of itinerant entertainers in the South Seas. The studio's first choices for the leads turned it down. Before long, the producer's thoughts turned to Bing Crosby and Bob Hope, as well as Dorothy Lamour in a sarong. Crosby and Hope were thought of together more and more as they traded jibes on the air. Movie moguls began to think that their rapport might work well on screen.

The moguls were proved right, but in a way that neither producer, director nor writer, nor especially fellow actors, could anticipate. It seemed that when Crosby and Hope were working together, the script was no more than a general guideline for the scene. The two ad libbed mercilessly. Poor Dorothy Lamour was allowed to slip in a line if and when she could find an opening. Fortunately, she had a good sense of humour.

Crosby and Hope made a game out of the work, injecting into the script a real sense of fun and spontaneity which made their work together brilliant and extraordinarily popular. The bottom line was that they were very, very funny.

When shooting of *The Road to Singapore* was finished, Hope worked into 1940 shooting the sequel to *The Cat and the Canary*, called *The Ghost Breakers*, again with Paulette Goddard.

Hope was asked to be the sole MC for the twelfth annual Academy Awards ceremony in February. The year's big winner was *Gone With the Wind*, with eight Oscars, including Best Picture, Director, Actress, and Supporting Actress. *Goodbye Mr. Chips* and *Stagecoach* also won awards. The competition was tough that year, with other classic films having been produced: *Wuthering Heights*, *Dark Victory*, *Of Mice and Men*, and *Mr. Smith Goes to Washington*.

In March, *The Road to Singapore* was released and proved to be an all-round hit. Paramount quickly looked for another script bringing together their now-famous trio of Hope, Crosby and Lamour and came up with *The Road to Zanzibar*.

Before shooting could begin, however, Bob had commitments to fill. He was due back on the road playing theatres around the country. The tour was enormously successful. Between his guarantee and a share of the ticket sales, Hope was making $20,000 a week. People were lining up around the block to see him. Bob and his agent Doc Shurr, who looked after his relations with Paramount, made sure that studio executives knew what a popular commodity they were working with.

Back in Hollywood, Hope, Crosby and Lamour filmed *The Road to Zanzibar*. Again, Crosby's and Hope's gagwriters were given private access to the script and the stars would show up and ad lib their way through the scenes. Even Dorothy Lamour got in on the act, showing up one day with a surprise smile: she had got the make-up people to blacken her teeth. It broke the boys up with laughter.

With *Zanzibar* Hope's stage and screen personality was now set. He had adopted the persona of a self-satisfied, leering, nervous type, who never succeeded in getting the girl, but always, somehow, got out of scrapes. A little too trustful, especially of the urbane Crosby, he made himself the butt of gag after gag, and the audience loved it.

Despite the giddiness that came with success, other events of 1940 cast a shadow over Bob's happiness. The war in Europe was creating ominous headlines. As Franklin D. Roosevelt ran for his unprecedented third term as President of the United States, Hitler's forces moved in and occupied France; the beaches of Dunkirk saw a dramatic rescue mounted from England; and the American military draft assembled the largest peace-time force ever. Bob worried about the Hope clan in England.

At home, though, there was good news. Little Linda was to celebrate her first birthday in July. Bob and Dolores decided that her birthday present would be a baby brother. Bob travelled by himself this time back to Evanston where he proudly became the father of Anthony (Tony). The baby endeared himself to his new dad by sporting his very own, tot-sized, ski-nose.

Dolores found herself taking most of the responsibility for rearing the children and maintaining the home, as Bob was working constantly. He was on the movie set for five days and then spent weekends rehearsing and preparing for the 'Pepsodent Show'. His schedule would become even more full and more hectic over the years, but Dolores rarely complained. Dolores admitted in a 1982 interview to having been lonely while her husband was so busy, but pointed out that wives of doctors, executives and soldiers face the same loneliness.[1]

To cap off the year, in December Bob celebrated his twentieth anniversary as an American citizen.

The next year, 1941, saw little break in Hope's full schedule. He completed three pictures. In *Caught in the Draft*, he was paired with Dorothy Lamour in a farce that had him accidently drafted into the army. It was released in Britain that summer and proved a great morale-booster there. Brave British citizens ignored air raids to attend round-the-clock showings. The bombed-out Coventry Cathedral in the Midlands was turned into an open-air theatre so that the city's homeless could have a laugh from Hope's outrageous comedy.

He also shot *Nothing But the Truth*, again with Paulette Goddard. Hope played a bashful stockbroker who bets that he can tell the absolute truth for 24 hours. In *Louisiana Purchase*, an Irving Berlin musical comedy, he was a filibustering Congressman.

The 'Pepsodent Show' went on the road in May for the first time. Bob had been asked to do the show from March Field Air Corps base at Riverside. Never one to lose an opportunity for good publicity, Bob took the show there at the time his military movie, *Caught in the Draft*, was released. Another enticement was the size of the audience – close to two thousand people. Hope has always loved a live audience.

The show proved so successful that it began a 35-year Hope tradition of entertaining the troops. It was the best radio audience he had ever had. His new studios became the Army, Navy, Air Force and Marine bases in the US. Between that show and 1948, all but two of Hope's radio programmes were broadcast from military bases. By the end of 1941, the *Motion Picture Daily* had named him the top radio star in the country, beating out Crosby and Jack Benny.

America was becoming increasingly concerned about the war during 1941. Although the country still was not militarily involved, the nation's mood was wary and defences were being built up. At the Academy Awards ceremony on 21 February 1941, Roosevelt spoke to the assembled crowd. He praised the movie industry for its contributions and its bolstering of patriotism and morale. He particularly gave credit to those celebrities who, like Hope, had begun to raise funds for agencies like the Red Cross, the March of Dimes, and European War Relief.

Again, Hope was the MC for the evening. The big winners that year were *Rebecca*, *The Grapes of Wrath*, and *The Philadelphia Story*, but it seemed that not just movies and screen performances were to be honoured that year. A stunned Bob Hope received a silver plaque from the Academy for 'Achievements in

Humanities', honouring him for his many benefits and for his 'unselfish services to the motion picture industry'.

Ironically, Hope was also gaining a reputation as a scrooge. *Time* Magazine profiled Hope on 7 July 1941, and said that 'if people grow weary of Hope's stylized impudence, it will be largely due to the star's appealing avarice ... Around the Paramount lot he is known as a "hard man with a dollar".'

Crosby came to his friend's defence with a letter to the magazine:

> My friend Bob Hope is anything but cheap. He does an average of two benefits a week. His price for a personal appearance would be about $10,000, so he gives away $20,000 every week of his life. Is that cheap?

Time responded: '*Time* agrees with Bing; however, Bob from time to time has been known to put undue pressure on a nickel.'

Hope's business sense was strong. In addition to maximizing his wages for his work, he encouraged Ivor to try to get defence contracts for their joint venture, Hope Metal Products. He also developed a gimmick with his sponsor, Pepsodent, to use his autobiography as a reward for purchasing their product. He wrote *They Got 'Em Covered*, a 95-page paperback (with the help of writers of course), and the book was given away to the radio show audience or sold for ten cents and a box top. His movies, radio show and book were all marketed together. Bob Hope had become an American product. His annual gross income was said to be over half a million dollars per year, though of course he had to pay a staff from that money as well as himself.

His last picture of the year 1941 was *My Favourite Blonde*. This time, Hope was the undisputed star. Bob played a man with a trained penguin who becomes the dupe of a beautiful spy. For this film he actually sang 'Thanks for the Memory' with the penguin. The film was unique for being the first to have a major celebrity in an unbilled walk-on part. The celebrity was none other than Crosby. It was also Bob's first foray as a leading man.

December 1941 has historical significance, though, far beyond the release of a milestone Bob Hope picture. The Japanese attacked Pearl Harbor. President Roosevelt used Bob's Pepsodent time-slot to make his second announcement of the

declaration of war. Hope's show was chosen because of the large
number of people who always tuned in at that time.

Bob plunged into the war effort with a vengeance. As almost half
a century has passed since then, it is not surprising that details of
some parts of Hope's life in the war years have become a little
muddled. For example, in his latest book, *Confessions of a
Hooker*, Bob recalls:

> On December 7, Bing [Crosby], Dick Gibson and I were
> staying at Elliot Roosevelt's home in Colorado Springs.
> When the news came from Pearl Harbor, we decided to join
> the Navy. Elliot got on the phone with his father in the
> White House and with Frank Knox, the Secretary of the
> Navy. Knox wanted to give us commissions in the Navy, but
> FDR said, "No, we don't want 'em in the Navy. We want
> 'em to do just what they're doing – entertaining the troops.'[2]

However, William Robert Faith, who wrote his doctoral disser-
tation on Bob Hope and had access to vast amounts of records
and many personal interviews, indicates that Bob heard the news
at home on the radio the day after appearing in Hollywood's
Santa Claus parade. Faith never mentions Hope's attempt to
enlist.[3]

Regardless of uncertainty about such details, the world knows
well what Bob Hope contributed to fund-raising and general
morale during the second World War and subsequent wars.
Perhaps even more important than his effect on overall public
morale was the boost he gave to thousands of Allied servicemen.

In 1942, Bob gave over 50 benefit performances, did an exhibition golf tour with Crosby for the Red Cross and other war
relief organizations and joined over 20 other major Hollywood
stars on the Hollywood Victory Caravan. The Victory Caravan
toured the United States raising money for the Army and Navy
Relief Fund. In addition, Hope filmed two movies, *Road to
Morocco* and *They Got Me Covered*. Each week he made his
Pepsodent radio broadcast, previewed before one military audience and then replayed for broadcast at another base, hence
actually two shows per week. As with the other 'Road' movies,
Road to Morocco starred Hope, Crosby and Lamour. It also

featured, for the third time, young Anthony Quinn, who as usual played the 'bad guy'.

The Victory Caravan was a 'whistle-stop' affair. The stars boarded a train on which they lived and rehearsed as they travelled from place to place giving shows, Hope was the MC as well as a performer in sketches. Some of the other famous names on this trip were Desi Arnaz, Charles Boyer, James Cagney, Claudette Colbert, Bing Crosby, Olivia de Havilland, Cary Grant, Bert Lahr, Laurel and Hardy, Groucho Marx, Merle Oberon, Eleanor Powell and Spencer Tracy.

When the troupe got to Washington, they attended a lawn party held by Eleanor Roosevelt. After a major performance in that city, they pressed on to Boston, Philadelphia and many other cities. Immediately after the two-week Victory Caravan, Hope made a four-week tour of military camps. He did 65 shows on that trip, as well as continuing his radio show.

In September, after shooting *They Got Me Covered*, Hope took off on a tour of military bases in Alaska, following the earlier lead of Al Jolson, Joe E. Brown and Edgar Bergen. Because of the weather, the small group of Hope and three other performers did most of their shows in overcrowded Quonset huts. During one flight they hit some very bad weather. The radio went out and there was no visibility. By a weird stroke of luck, another plane passed by close enough for them to feel the air currents. That plane, whose radio was operating normally, informed the people at the nearest air base, who lit powerful searchlights to guide the pilots down. Everyone was safe, but to Hope and the others it had seemed as if their careers were about to come to an abrupt end. They had even donned their parachutes and life jackets.

In this early military work, Hope learned that the troops liked best the jokes that made fun of themselves and the often dismal circumstances in which they found themselves. Hope always made a point of learning something about his audience and their circumstances before each show.

Next on Hope's 1942 agenda was a movie based on the play, *Let's Face It*, which ran on Broadway for about a year. The play starred Danny Kaye and Eve Arden and was written by Herbert and Dorothy Fields and Cole Porter. Sam Goldwyn wanted to make the film with Bob Hope, but he balked at the amount of money Doc Shurr was trying to get for his client.

During the delay, Hope was the MC in *Star Spangled Rhythm*, an extravaganza that starred what seemed like half of the stars from Hollywood's skies. He also continued his radio broadcasts from military bases around the country.

Goldwyn finally gave in. Recognizing Hope's enormous popular appeal, he paid him another $100,000 to make *Let's Face It*. His co-stars were Eve Arden, Betty Hutton and Zasu Pitts.

In early 1943, Hope was invited to put his prints in the cement sidewalk in front of Grauman's Chinese movie theatre. Hope not only made impressions of his hands and feet, he carried through and immortalized his famous nose in the cement.

Hope was again the MC at the Academy Awards ceremony. *Mrs Miniver* was the big winner, earning Best Picture, Best Director and Best Actress (Greer Garson). Crosby's 'White Christmas' won Best Song. The audience was filled with uniforms, as the result of more and more actors enlisting. That night, Tyrone Power and Alan Ladd, both in uniform, brought a flag with the names of the more than 26,500 film industry personnel who had joined the war cause.

Hope worried that people would think ill of him for not having joined the fray (although his civilian contribution to the war effort was already great). His friend Ed Sullivan, still a columnist at the time, posed the question to his readers. Nearly everyone who wrote in thought Hope should be deferred.

Another kind of publicity came from across the Atlantic. In April, 1943, a columnist in London wrote an open letter to Hope asking him to come back to Great Britain to perform.

Immediately following a ten-week tour in the US that spring, Bob set off to do a USO tour in Europe. He started in London, and from there made a short trip to Hitchin to see Grandfather James, now 99 years old. The USO tour in England lasted five weeks, sometimes involving appearances in four different places in one day. Hope went to the hospitals, the supply depots and anywhere there were fighting men needing cheer. For their part they stood in the rain for him and crowded into tiny halls to see him, and his jokes were told and retold in the barracks and the hospital wards.

Life in England was still difficult but there was hope in the air. The Drive for Victory had started and the German Afrika Korps had been defeated. The Germans were being driven out of Russia and the Allies were bombing German cities.

The USO tour moved through England and into Wales, then returned to London. They played Colchester in Essex and Bob arranged for his grandfather to see the show. The old man rose from his sickbed and actually appeared on stage with his famous grandson. Sadly, not long afterward, on 22 July, he passed away. He had lived a long and full life and had been proud of his American grandson.

Following a three-day stint in Northern Ireland, the tour finished in London. One of the highlights was an opportunity to meet Winston Churchill. That same day, an enormously gratifying article appeared in the London *Daily Express*. It was written by the novelist John Steinbeck, who was then working for the New York *Herald Tribune* (which printed the story on 20 July 1943). The article was picked up by papers around the world, and appeared on 31 July in London. In it Steinbeck wrote: 'When the time for recognition of service to the nation in wartime comes to be considered, Bob Hope should be high on the list.'[4] And he went on to describe Hope's role as being an important bridge between America and her fighting men.

Hope and company waited in Scotland for transport to North Africa. On reaching Algiers, Hope found himself sweltering in the heavy clothes he had brought for England. A colonel lent him a green suit which he wore for the next four weeks of his tour. These audiences were combat-hardened and tough, but they loved Hope and his group, who were frequently in danger from air raids, bombs and tracer bullets and were beginning to feel combat-hardened themselves.

On 18 August 1943, the Allies invaded Sicily. Hope was due to fly to Palermo on 21 August and went ahead with it. The trip brought Hope as close to death as he would probably ever get in entertaining the troops. The Germans dive-bombed the Hope group's hotel, machine guns blasting. The Allies responded. The noise was deafening. Plaster fell from the ceilings and everyone was scared out of their wits. Luckily, they came out of it shaken but unscathed.

Back in Algiers after the Palermo incident, they were working on a radio show script when they were told that General Eisenhower would like to meet them. Hope was very impressed with 'Ike' and would remember the visit for a long time.

That night, Algiers was hit by its worst bombing raid ever. Hope's group spent the attack in an air raid shelter. The next day they gladly returned to England. Bob was carrying autographed pictures from General Eisenhower, General Patton and General Doolittle.

The intrepid performers finally headed home after a journey of 20,000 miles and countless performances. Although Hope was not the only entertainer to give shows for the troops or even travel close to the battle lines, he was singled out for his efforts because of the sheer volume of what he did and his willingness and exuberance in doing it. From the foxholes to the burn wards, from frozen Quonset huts to broiling tents, before audiences of two to two thousand, Bob Hope raised hopes around the world. He brought a touch of home, reminded the weary soldiers of what it was they were fighting for, and gave of himself past the point of exhaustion.

Time Magazine featured Hope on its cover on 20 September 1943. The accompanying article was called 'Hope for Humanity', and identified Hope as a 'legend'. Bob had quickly become a folk hero. Perhaps it was because despite his mugging and his obvious ego, Hope was genuinely sincere in his respect and admiration for fighting men. He honoured these men and showed it through affectionate insults and self-deprecation. His method earned him laughs and love.

Naturally, Hope went right back to work in Los Angeles. His Pepsodent radio show began another season and was the most listened-to show in the nation. He began writing a book about his experiences overseas with the help of Carroll Carroll. Called *I Never Left Home*, it was finished in December. Hope also did two or three benefit performances a week and, in November, went back to work with Dorothy Lamour and Bing Crosby on the next *Road* picture. This one was called *The Road to Utopia*.

The Road to Utopia required more stunts than any of the former pictures. Some of these were quite dangerous, including one with a 'trained' bear. The bear didn't quite cooperate and its growling caused both Hope and Crosby to refuse to work with the animal. They were right to have refused, for the bear seriously mauled its trainer the next day. Between German warplanes and Paramount stunts, 1943 was without doubt Bob Hope's most dangerous year.

Given the Hays Office restrictions of the day, the film was quite daring. For once, Hope gets the girl. The final scene takes place several years later, with Bing coming back to see the two. Hope and Lamour proudly introduce their son – and he is the spitting image of Crosby. Pretty risqué for the time.

In 1944, Hope continued his gruelling schedule, but found himself fighting off a nasty cold for weeks. Whenever Dolores could get a good look at him she would force him to come home or to Palm Springs to rest. He hosted the annual Gridiron Dinner, broadcasting it on the Pepsodent show. This event is sponsored and attended by journalists. The guest being 'roasted' that year was President Roosevelt, and Hope earned enormous laughs, along with the others, with his jokes about the President. People began to compare Bob to the deceased Will Rogers.

In April, 1944, he made a picture for Sam Goldwyn called *The Princess and the Pirate*. It was to be Hope's last film for a year, largely because of a salary dispute with Paramount. Hope wanted to form his own production company to keep more of the money he was earning from his highly popular movies. It was a long fight in an era when studios still felt they owned their stars' lives.

The last Pepsodent show of the season was broadcast on 6 June 1944. This was also D-Day, when more than 4,000 ships backed by 11,000 planes, carrying brave men from England, Canada and America, landed on the shores of Normandy.

Meanwhile, the savage war in the Pacific theatre continued. On 22 June Hope and company set off to entertain the soldiers, sailors and marines in that dangerous zone. From Hawaii, they flew in General MacArthur's personal plane to Christmas Island. Gary Cooper had been there the year before, and for most of the troops stationed there, that had been the last glimpse of home. The island was infested with rodents and vicious insects. There was no fresh water. The Hope group continued performing from island to island until exhaustion set in. Finally, they decided to take a break in Australia.

What should have been the safest part of the trip turned out to be the most dangerous. Near the end of the all-day flight, one of the plane's engines simply quit. The troupe threw out all their luggage and personal effects, even the plane's tools. The pilot put down the pontoons and managed to land them on a river. They evacuated the craft immediately. Local residents had seen the plane coming down and came to help. They came from the little town of Laurieton, where a grateful Hope put on a special show for them.

By the time the troupe finally got to Sydney, news had been

broadcast that their plane had gone down. Thousands of cheering fans greeted them. All in all, this trip took them 30,000 miles and encompassed 150 performances. Hope recorded much of the journey in a series of articles sent back to American newspapers. His legend continued to grow.

6

The Laughter of the World

In 1945, Bob Hope was riding high. His Pepsodent radio show was doing so well that he signed a new ten-year contract for about a million dollars a year. His number-one rated show was selling a lot of toothpaste. The show was a full six rating points above his nearest competitor, *Fibber McGee*.

He continued writing his column, which was published in papers around the country. As usual, he supervised and approved the actual writing. Bob made more tours of US military bases, then returned to Europe for another tour. He entertained for three months in England, France, Germany, Austria and Czechoslovakia. In addition, he continued to do benefits and appeared with other stars in programmes to support the war effort.

Hope again hosted the Academy Awards ceremony, which was broadcast live on radio. To his surprise, the evening began with a special presentation as Bob was given lifetime membership in the Academy. The year's big winner was a Crosby project called *Going My Way*. This movie won awards for Best Director (Leo McCarey), Actor (Bing) and Supporting Actor (Barry Fitzgerald) as well as the coveted Best Picture. The beautiful Ingrid Bergman took the Best Actress statue for *Gaslight*, and Ethel Barrymore won Best Supporting Actress for *None But the Lonely Heart*.

Not long afterwards, on 12 April 1945, America's longest-serving President, Franklin Delano Roosevelt, died of a cerebral haemorrhage. Hope joined the nation in mourning. He felt Roosevelt had been a great humanitarian worthy of everyone's respect, and he honoured his ability to rally his fellow citizens around the causes he believed in.

The war in Europe finally ended a few days later, on 8 May
1945. The Pacific war continued, however, and Bob didn't stop
supporting the war effort. On 12 May, he took his radio show to
Washington for a three-hour special to sell war bonds. His popularity encouraged a total of $2.5 million in pledges. While in the
capital, he was asked to entertain at the White House, where
President Truman gave him a personal tour of his new home.

Still in Washington, Bob received one of the greatest honours
ever bestowed on him. His statue had been sculpted and placed
in the Smithsonian's 'Living Hall of Fame'.

Hope continued his bond drive around the country, frequently
using exhibition golf matches as a means to raise funds. Crosby
joined him often.

When Bob left for his three-month long tour of Europe that
summer, he had the pleasure of crossing on the *Queen Mary*,
once again a passenger ship. On Independence Day, he was in
London performing at the Albert Hall. A riot nearly started as
GIs scrambled across and over season ticket holders to grab
whatever seats they could. Over a thousand people had to be
locked outside. There was no room to let them in to see one of
America's favourite sons on America's most patriotic day.

Shortly afterwards, as Bob was performing in Germany, word
arrived that the Japanese were offering to surrender. World War
II was nearly over.

Bob Hope came home to the Paramount lot. With the help of his
agents, the dilemma over Hope Enterprises was finally resolved.
Paramount agreed to let this new firm co-produce Hope's films.

Hope's first film after his year-long break from moviedom was
a comic remake of Rudolph Valentino's 1924 film *Monsieur
Beaucaire*. Work on the picture was complicated by a number
of production problems, including a dispute over who would
write the script, as well as elaborate stunts and gimmicks. In
previews, it didn't seem funny enough, so new slapstick scenes
were shot and edited in. It worked. The result was a very funny
and successful film.

Hope immediately began his next film, *Where There's Life*, in
which he plays a radio star tapped to be king of a fictitious
European country. He spends most of the movie evading the
'messengers' who've come to take him there.

Stories were beginning to circulate about Hope's wealth.

Between his movie fees, personal appearances, radio show, newspaper column, investments and Hope Metal Products, he was said to take in over $1.35 million dollars per year. Despite all this, Bob found himself cash-poor. His income taxes tended to be enormous.

Another problem was that his radio show was losing its audience. The long emphasis on the military had turned off the civilians. Fortunately, that audience didn't stay away for long.

Hope went on tour in the summer of 1946 to earn the money to pay his taxes. On the tour, he stopped in Bing Crosby's hometown, Spokane, Washington. Spokane put a couple of blots on Hope's image of all-round good guy. The 'halo' began to dim a little, a trend that continued through the later Vietnam era. Hope lost none of his overall popularity, but some people were looking beyond the publicity.

A reporter for the Spokane *Post-Intelligencer* wanted to write about Hope the Businessman. Reports had circulated about his two new corporations (besides Hope Enterprises, he had a corporation to handle his personal appearances) and about his reputed wealth. The reporter talked to Doc Shurr, who refused to answer any financial questions about Hope, but was denied an interview with Hope himself. He wrote an article focusing on the size of Hope's entourage and implying Hope's staff functioned as an obsequious claque. It wasn't too different from the early days in Cleveland when Hope had packed the audience at amateur contents.

Another disturbing incident involved his brother Jim. Unknown to Bob or to Jim, they were both performing in Spokane at the same time. A reporter made them aware of it, and asked Jim if he and his wife (with whom he performed) would pose for pictures with the more famous member of the family. They readily agreed, and a time and place was chosen. Bob never showed up. Jim waited for hours. The two never got together, nor even spoke , although Bob sent Doc Shurr to watch his brother's act.

His relationship with his other brothers was better. Sadly, one of them was near the end. As his tour wound down, Bob got word that his brother Sid was dying of the cancer he had been fighting for a long time.

Bob was with Secretary of War Harry Goodring when he got the news. Goodring immediately arranged for a Navy plane to fly

Bob to Columbus to pick up his brother Fred and then go on to Toledo, which was near Sid's home.

Sid was a quiet man who had preferred country life. He was married and had five children. He was just 41 years old, two years younger than Bob. Bob was able to have a good visit with Sid, who was still able to be up and around. Sid asked Bob to watch over his children after he died.

Bob returned to Los Angeles and began shooting *My Favourite Brunette* to follow up on the success of his earlier *My Favourite Blonde*. The picture co-starred Dorothy Lamour with Peter Lorre and Lon Chaney, Jr. Crosby showed up for a cameo at the end.

In August, during the filming of this movie, Sid passed away. Bob chartered a plane to take the West Coast contingent of the Hope family to the funeral.

Awards were becoming an almost routine fact of Bob Hope's life. He had already received quite a number, including a day in Philadelphia called Bob Hope Day. That autumn, the list continued to grow. The American Legion gave him their Distinguished Service Medal. In Washington, General Eisenhower presented him with the country's highest civilian award, the Medal of Merit. It was given in recognition of Hope's wartime efforts, especially his entertaining of the troops. Following the ceremony, Hope went to the White House to see Truman.

A subsequent presentation awarded Bob and Dolores an even greater honour. The Cradle had approved the Hopes for another baby. Dolores met Bob in Chicago and they went to the orphanage together.

They had a huge surprise. In addition to the two-month-old baby girl they had been promised, there was also an infant boy. Bob quickly signed the papers for both and the family was now complete with the addition of Nora and Kelly.

At the end of 1945, Hope published his third book, *So This Is Peace*, again written with Carroll Carroll. Mostly comedy material, it was quickly a best-seller.

It was time for another *Road* picture, this time *The Road to Rio*. Crosby and Hope each owned a third of the movie. This gave them the opportunity to promote a new product they had invested in. Each man had put $25,000 into a company out of Alabama called Lime Cola in hopes of overtaking Coca-Cola. In *The Road to Rio*, they put up Lime Cola signs all over the set. Before the film was released, the company went out of business. Watching the movie with all those Lime Cola signs was not a pleasant experience for either of the two friends.

During the shoot, Bob MC'd a special broadcast for Paramount. The studio had just launched a new television station and produced a 'spectacular' to get things moving. Very, very few homes had sets to view the show, which was just as well, since it wasn't a great show. Bob remained sceptical of the new medium.

Censorship was still a big issue in Hollywood then, not only in the movies but also on radio. Fred Allen had a regular Sunday night programme on NBC. Allen told a joke about a fictional NBC vice-president and was cut off the air for ten seconds. Hope referred to the episode on his Tuesday night show and he, too, was cut off for six seconds. That same night, Red Skelton referred to the incident and was censored as well. It happened again two weeks later to Hope when he told his guest, Frank Sinatra, that he would be joining him on his show on CBS. Finally, NBC's president apologized to all involved and recommended that Allen, Skelton and Hope all be made honorary vice-presidents of NBC.

After a South American vacation, Hope returned to make *The Paleface* with Jane Russell. It was to be his biggest box-office hit.

Jane Russell's first film had been *The Outlaw*, produced by Howard Hughes. The movie shocked the public with the view it gave of Miss Russell's exceptional cleavage. The movie was seen briefly in both 1941 and 1943, but not released to full distribution until 1950. In the meantime, she had made a reputation. Bob Hope once introduced her as 'the two and only Miss Russell'. *The Paleface*, released in 1948, was only her third film.

Hope's radio contract with Pepsodent was approaching hard times. His 1947 season opener got poor reviews. However, this didn't bother Hope much. He was still at the top of the ratings, still earning honours and accolades, including a Friar's Roast. He was invited to appear at a Command Performance at London's Palladium Theatre to follow the marriage of Princess Elizabeth to Philip Mountbatten. He was also invited to attend the wedding. Hope planned to prerecord parts of his radio show and then perform the monologue live from that famous stage.

The Command Performance was a huge success. Hope entertained for the British royalty, as well as the Queen of Denmark and the King of Romania. Hope met King George (Elizabeth's father) and joked with the monarch.

From England, Hope went on to do a tour of Germany. He was becoming ill, and exhaustion was slowing him down and taking away his voice. Still, the grateful occupation forces cheered him on.

Hope flew back to New York after stopping in England to smooth things over with his sponsors. He returned to Palm Springs for a rest, where his doctor told him to restrict his activities to the radio show. Bob tried to cut down, but found he had committed himself to a number of benefits which he insisted on completing.

At a news conference in the autumn of 1947, Hope found that his views on foreign policy were nearly as interesting to the reporters as his next movie. He was widely quoted for his enthusiastic comments on the Marshall Plan, which he urged all Americans to support in order to aid the economic recovery of Europe and maintain America's friendship with the Western European nations.

As the end of the 1940s approached, radio was facing a tough new competitor: television. To pep up the appeal of his radio show, Hope hired on Doris Day as a regular, along with the Les Brown Band.

Doris Day had been born Doris von Kappelhoff in 1924. She changed her name after she became a singer, choosing 'Day' from one of her songs, 'Day by Day'. She sang with the Les Brown Band. Her first film, made in 1948, was *Romance on the High Seas*, and following that her film career took off in earnest. The cheerful star we all know for her roles opposite Rock Hudson and others in light romantic comedies had endured many bad breaks and personal problems. She had been hospitalized for a year at 13; was in a car accident at 15 that ended her dancing career; had gone on the road at 16; married a man she described as a 'psychopath' musician at 17; and married again unsuccessfully at 22. She performed beautifully on Hope's show, but later confessed that she had been terrified before all the live performances.

The autumn of 1948 saw a presidential election. Hope's humour was growing more and more political. After the Dewey defeat, Hope wired Harry Truman a brief message. It said, simply, 'Unpack'.

The night of Hope's first radio show of the new season was also marked by the premiere appearance of Milton Berle as MC of *The Texaco Star Theatre* on television. Hope Enterprises began to look at television more seriously.

As Christmas of 1948 approached, Bob planned a family event at Lake Tahoe. That plan changed, though, when he got a call from his golfing buddy, Stuart Symington, Secretary of the Air Force. Symington asked Hope, on behalf of President Truman, to do a Christmas tour for the GIs in Germany. American forces were then engaged in distributing food and coal to the now-isolated Berliners. Hope agreed.

Symington sent his plane for Bob and Dolores, as well as for the Vice-President, General Jimmy Doolittle, a few Rockettes from Radio City, Irving Berlin (composer of 'White Christmas') and a few others. Hope, with Pepsodent's blessing this time, planned to do his radio broadcast from Berlin. Once again, the lonely soldiers were happy to see him and recognized the risks he had taken to come to them.

Back home, the ratings of Hope's radio show began to falter. He took the cast on the road again for a 36-city tour. His latest picture, *The Paleface*, opened to enormous enthusiasm. People lined up around the block to see him cavort, in technicolour, with the luscious Jane Russell.

The tour netted Hope a whopping $700,000, or $11,000 a day. He needed the money to start his next picture, *Fancy Pants*, although people were calling him a millionaire now. In *Fancy Pants*, Bob co-starred with the carrot-topped Lucille Ball. Lucy established herself early in Hollywood. She made dozens of films in the 1940s, starting in bit and supporting roles and finally achieving co-star status. She married the Cuban bandleader Desi Arnaz in 1941.

Fancy Pants was Hope's second movie with Lucille Ball. Earlier in the year, the two were in *Sorrowful Jones*, a so-so remake of 1934's *Little Miss Marker* and one of Hope's more serious roles.

During the filming of *Fancy Pants*, Hope had an accident. The script called for Lucy to teach him to ride a horse. They didn't use a real horse, but rather a bucking barrel, similar to the mechanical bulls popular later in Texas singles bars. Poor Bob fell off the thing and was rushed to hospital. There was nothing seriously wrong with him, fortunately, but he was badly bruised and had to stay in hospital for a week.

During the summer of 1949, Bob and Bing Crosby added to their net worth with a venture into oil wells. Bob met a man at a Fort Worth benefit who suggested the investment. Bing agreed to join in the $50,000 outlay. The first well brought up salt water, but the two remained optimists and doubled their investment. They were proved right, and hit a gusher that promised to earn them close to $3.5 million each.

As Hope started his twelfth (and last) radio season for Pepsodent, he became increasingly interested in television. Television people had been approaching him for a long time, but he had turned down their offers. Now Sid Caesar and Imogene Coca could be seen in *Broadway Revue* each week. The show was well-produced and funny. TV began to look more attractive. Hope asked Jimmy Saphier to talk to General Motors about a proposition the company had made to him earlier.

His timing was certainly right. In 1949 there were 127 TV stations and approximately two million sets in use. Milton Berle, in his second season, was gaining popularity. Hope himself was, according to a Gallup Poll, far and away the most popular comedian in any medium in the country, and movie production had slowed down.

While negotiations went on and Hope continued on radio, he made another movie, *The Great Lover*. At the time of its release, *Motion Picture Daily* announced that Bob Hope was the leading box office draw in the country.

At times in his career, cynics have regarded Hope's benefits and GI entertainment tours as self-serving publicity-hunting – even in the face of the obvious risks and the exhausting schedule he kept up. But at Christmas of 1949, not even the worst cynic could accuse Bob of anything other than good-heartedness.

At the last minute, Stu Symington and Brigadier General Frank Armstrong (who had just had his real-life story portrayed in the new film, *Twelve O'Clock High*) convinced him to join them on a tour of Alaskan bases. Bob agreed, with less than four hours to organize a troupe and pack up the family. The two youngest children, Kelly and Nora, stayed home, but Dolores and the very excited Linda and Tony quickly got ready and went off with three other performers. The tour involved doing twelve shows in three days. Dolores even joined Bob on stage.

In early 1950 Hope was involved in another accident, this time while driving. Although it could have been fatal or permanently damaging, Bob was not seriously hurt. His car went out of control on a rainy highway, skidded into a ditch, flipped over and smashed into a tree. His companion was bruised, and Hope suffered a fractured collar-bone. A lucky escape, but it curtailed Bob's golf game for quite a while.

While he was recuperating, the Frigidaire division of General Motors came through with a TV deal that was too good to refuse. Bob signed a contract to do five shows for a total of $150,000. The money was his personal appearance fee and guest stars and production costs would be paid by the sponsor. It was an exceptional sum at the time and caused quite a stir. The first show was scheduled for Easter. It would be on NBC, as was his radio show (now falling rapidly in the ratings).

Before his TV debut, Bob did another vaudeville stint, hiring Jane Russell and the Les Brown Band to accompany him. Because of heavy publicity and clever gimmicks, he brought in huge audiences for all the shows he performed during the two weeks. At this time, he took on the job of heading up fundraising for the effort to combat cerebral palsy. He also hired a young singer named Antonio Benedetti, thus launching Tony Bennett's career.

Finally it was time for the first TV show. The *Star Spangled Revue*, as the 90 minute special was called, included Bea Lillie, Douglas Fairbanks, Jr and Dinah Shore as guests. The reviews were mixed and Hope himself was displeased with his performance. For some reason, the seasoned trouper had been very nervous and it showed.

His next TV show, a Mother's Day special, included Frank Sinatra as the guest, as well as the singer Peggy Lee. This time things went better. Hope was adjusting to the moving cameras, the technicians and the general activity that went on during the live show. He adjusted by laying down the law and forbidding unnecessary moving around. It made his work easier and the performances turned out much better.

Lever Brothers, the manufacturers of Pepsodent, now wanted to cancel Hope's radio contract. They had had a number of differences with him, the most serious being Bob's wish to record the show against the sponsor's insistence that it be done live. Bob sued and the case went as far as the Supreme Court.

Bob lost. Fortunately, his agents had secured a deal directly with NBC that took effect at about the same time. He now had an independent exclusive contract with the network. A better deal financially, it netted him nearly a million dollars a year.

While reconstruction from World War II was still going on, the United States discovered a new reason for putting its young men in uniform. The situation in Korea had deteriorated into armed conflict, though war was never officially declared. General Douglas MacArthur was given command of the new United Nations 'peacekeeping' forces.

During the first weeks of what became known as the Korean War, Hope finished work on his next movie, *The Lemon Drop Kid*, a Damon Runyon story. He went on to make his third TV show, then packed his bags and got ready to entertain the troops again.

Starting in Hawaii and jumping from island to island in the South Pacific, Hope and company soon reached Korea. It was freezing and it was dangerous. And once, because of a foul-up in communications, the entertainers actually arrived at a site before the military did. Hope had beaten the Marines to the beach. While on the way Hope taped his radio show. After a promotional tour of Japan, the group headed home.

At the end of 1950 *The Lemon Drop Kid* was released. Memorable for introducing the now-standard Christmas song, 'Silver Bells', the film made Crosby's recording of the song the most widely sold and played of that time.

Hope had been keeping up a breakneck pace. He was on radio, television, movies, and stage (both for money and for benefits); he continued his newspaper column and he oversaw his business interests. He might be recognized as the most travelled American in history if it were possible to calculate his mileage. Throughout the 1950s, Hope's life and career continued unabated. Bob worked on, motivated by a desire for the money he earned, a need to hear the applause, and a genuine love of his lifestyle.

In 1951, he filmed *My Favourite Spy* with Hedy Lamarr. He toured the music halls of England and Scotland for two weeks, a task he would repeat many times during the rest of his career. He played in countless golf tournaments. He received the USO's highest honour from Harry Truman.

In 1952, Hope went back to the studios to film *Son of Paleface* with Jane Russell, Roy Rogers and his horse, Trigger. Not much later, Bob was on the *Road* again, this time in *The Road to Bali*.

The Road to Bali was the first *Road* picture in five years, and the first of the series in Technicolor. Hope also made *Off Limits* with Mickey Rooney and *Here Come the Girls*, a musical with Rosemary Clooney and Arlene Dahl.

Bob was now on television once a month for the *Colgate Comedy Hour*. His ratings were enough to convince General Foods, the manufacturer, to sign him to a lucrative three-year exclusive contract. In addition he successfully ran for president of the American Guild of Variety Artists (AGVA).

Besides his regular benefit appearances, Hope continued as honorary chairman for the Cerebral Palsy Fund and gave considerable time to raising money for the Boy Scouts and the Damon Runyon Cancer Fund.

Although Bob had long been friends with various military big-wigs and important people in politics, 1952 saw him become more personally involved in political activity. That year, Dwight D. Eisenhower ran for President of the United States. Hope had long been an admirer of the General. Because of Hope's position as a spokesman for consumer products, he rarely came out positively on either side of a political question. In 1952, however, NBC cast him as a guest commentator at both the Republican and Democratic national conventions. He gave short monologues each night using political humour.

In 1952 and 1953, the United States saw the rise of a politician whom history has judged a bully and a villain, the junior senator from Wisconsin, Joe McCarthy. McCarthy perceived Communist spies everywhere – or claimed to perceive them. He manipulated his Senate Committee and its televised proceedings to create a nationwide epidemic of fear and suspicion. The Hollywood community was particulary hard-hit by the anti-Communist paranoia. Suspected Communists, including those who merely refused to identify other suspects, were blacklisted. It took many of them a number of years to rebuild their careers. And for some, it ended their careers.

Hope was not a fan of McCarthy, unlike Ronald Reagan and others. He also knew that Ike didn't care for the Senator either. Bob began making barbed comments about the McCarthy accusations. They weren't particularly strong except in comparison to his usual hands-off policy on political matters. Neverthe-

less Hope did get some critical letters from Americans hyper-
sensitive to 'Reds' in their midst. Here's an example of Hope's
anti-McCarthy jokes:

On a December, 1952, television show, reading a letter from
Santa Claus: 'Thank you for . . . the beautiful new brown suit . . .
But tell Senator McCarthy I'm going to wear my old red one
anyway . . . I had it first.'[1]

Months later the Senator was finally judged by the majority of
the public to be an arrogant demagogue.

Hope and Eisenhower became good friends, not least because
they shared a common passion – golf. They played many games
together. Hope always kept his ribbing about Ike affectionate.

Settling down from extensive touring, Bob had time for some
business, including buying part of radio station KOA in Denver.
He sat down with a writer by the name of Pete Martin, who had
helped Bing Crosby write his autobiography, and started his
own. The book had a long title: *Have Tux, Will Travel: Bob
Hope's Own Story, as told to Pete Martin.* Profits from the book
were earmarked for the Bob and Dolores Hope Foundation,
which was set up to handle all the requests he received for
charitable contributions, and to the Cerebral Palsy Fund.

Unlike the current trend toward tell-all celebrity biographies
such as *Mommie Dearest*, the book told Hope's life story in a
somewhat idealized and superficial manner.

Hope hosted the Academy Awards again in 1953. Best Picture
that year went to *The Greatest Show on Earth*, Gary Cooper was
named Best Actor for his role in *High Noon* and Shirley Booth
took the best actress award for *Come Back, Little Sheba*. The
young actor who had started as the villain in the *Road* pictures
took Best Supporting Actor: Anthony Quinn won for his part in
Viva Zapata!.

These were great movies and great performances, but the 1953
Oscars were most notable for being televised for the first time.
With Hope making his seventh appearance as MC, NBC paid for
and broadcast the event. The TV audience got to see Hope
receive his third award from the Academy. Still not even nominated for his performance, he was given an Oscar for 'his contribution to the laughter of the world, his service to the motion
picture industry, and his devotion to the American premise'.

Bob's movie that year was called *Casanova's Big Night*. His co-stars were Joan Fontaine and Basil Rathbone. Hope's next movie tested his acting abilities, but it was a role for which his background clearly suited him. It was *The Seven Little Foys*, a biography of vaudeville star Eddie Foy.

The film wasn't the first movie to portray Foy's life. His son, Eddie Foy, Jr., portrayed his father in various films: *Frontier Marshal* (1939), *Lillian Russell* (1940), *Yankee Doodle Dandy* (1942), and *Wilson* (1944).

Eddie Foy, Sr. had been a very popular vaudevillian. Unfortunately, his pleasantness on stage did not carry over to his home behaviour. When his wife died, Foy took his seven reluctant children and put them on stage. Foy was a very good dancer, and Hope went into training to be able to portray him. He engaged the services of his old idol, Nick Castle, to help both him and Jimmy Cagney (who had agreed to play the small part of George M. Cohan). Cagney and Hope created one of Hollywood's most memorable scenes when they danced a challenge duet together.

Cagney had refused pay for his part in the film because of the hospitality he had received from the Foys in his youth. Eddie Foy, Jr. narrated the film and two other of the now-grown Foys gave advice. Bob relied on his own experience to act the vaudeville scenes.

Not all reviews were ecstatic, but most were generally good. Hope was given credit for his real ability to act, as critics noted that he was playing a character other than himself for once, and doing a fine job of it.

7

Splendid American

Hope's monthly television show continued to draw a large audience during the 1954 season, but many critics were disappointed by what they called the 'sameness' of his humour. His style and manner had never really changed, despite his use of current events.

His invitation that autumn to give a Royal Command Performance in London was an invitation to change. Bob decided to originate his TV show from London and make it an 'international revue' for the American audience. At the same time, he could do the performance for the Queen. The show, filmed at the BBC studios, included Maurice Chevalier and the usual bevy of beautiful women. Bob had succeeded in giving American TV that 'something different' that had been missing from his earlier shows.

His next movie was *That Certain Feeling*, adapted from the Broadway show *King of Hearts*. Pearl Bailey sang the title song, and Hope's co-star was Eva Marie Saint. This was only her second movie, but the year before she had won an Oscar for Best Supporting Actress for her role opposite Marlon Brando in *On the Waterfront*. (The Academy also honoured *On the Waterfront* with awards for Best Picture, Director and Actor.) But *That Certain Feeling* was not one of Hope's better films, and many people in fact found it surprisingly bad.

The production of Hope's next movie led to a public controversy between Hope and the writers of the film. Because he was so frequently performing in England, Hope agreed to make a film there which was eventually titled *The Iron Petticoat*.

Cary Grant had turned down this film, and its writer, Ben Hecht, had turned to Hope. Hope was to co-star with Katharine

Hepburn, who had had her ups and downs in Hollywood. Her screen debut had been in *A Bill of Divorcement*, which was a big hit. She had won her first Academy Award for her third picture, *Morning Glory*, and after a slump, appeared opposite Cary Grant twice in 1938, in *Bringing Up Baby* and *Holiday*. Branded 'box office poison' by studio executives, she went back to Broadway where she had a hit with a play called *The Philadelphia Story*. She negotiated the movie rights to the play and returned to the screen in it with Cary Grant and Jimmy Stewart. This film broke all attendance records at Radio City Music Hall and earned her another Academy Award nomination. Some of her better films between *The Philadelphia Story* and her appearance with Hope were *Woman of the Year, Adam's Rib, The African Queen*, and *Pat and Mike*.

There were some problems with the script of *The Iron Petticoat*, so Hope, as usual, brought in his own writers to beef it up. Their work was close to a rewrite, which made Hecht furious. He took out a full-page ad with his own money in *The Hollywood Reporter* to address an open letter to Hope in October, 1956. It said:

> My dear partner Bob Hope,
>   This is to notify you that I have removed my name as author from our mutilated venture, *The Iron Petticoat*.
>   Unfortunately, your other partner, Katharine Hepburn, can't shy out of the fractured picture with me.
>   Although her magnificent comic performance has been blowtorched out of the film, there is enough left of the Hepburn footage to identify her for the sharpshooters.
>   I am assured by my hopeful predators that *The Iron Petticoat* will go over big with people 'who can't get enough of Bob Hope.'
>   Let us hope this swooning contingent is not confined to yourself and your euphoric agent, Louis Shurr.
>
> > Yours anonymously,
> > Ben Hecht

Hecht was a highly respected writer who did not care much for the Hollywood 'scene'. He had received two Oscars for Best Screenplay, including the first ever awarded, and he had written the scripts for such distinguished films as *The Front Page*,

Scarface, Gunga Din, Wuthering Heights, and *Notorious*. It wasn't surprising that his style and Hope's didn't mesh.

An equally annoyed Hope responded to Hecht's attack with his own open letter:

> My dear ex-partner, Ben,
>
> I am most understanding. The way things are going you simply can't afford to be associated with a hit.
>
> As for Kate Hepburn, I don't think she was depressed with the preview audience rave about her performance.
>
> Let's do all our correspondence this way in future . . . in print.
>
> > Yours,
> > Bob (Blow-Torch) Hope

Hope and Hepburn got along fairly well on the set and no evidence exists that she joined in this battle. But, with the perspective of time, it seems odd that anyone ever tried to mix the styles of these two movie stars. The critics were rather kind, all things considered.

Hope's next film was another biography, that of the colourful mayor of New York, Jimmy Walker. The movie was called *Beau James*, with Hope in the title role. It was a straight drama – no gags, no jokes, no slapstick. The cast included Vera Miles, Paul Douglas, Alexis Smith and Darren McGavin. The film was narrated by Walter Winchell and there were brief appearances by Jimmy Durante, Jack Benny and George Jessel. It was Hope's last serious film, and was fairly well received.

That same year, 1957, Hope also made *Paris Holiday*. He originated the idea for the script and produced the film himself. It was shot in France with Anita Ekberg and the non-English-speaking actor Fernandel. The film went way over budget, and anxiety mounted among all involved when Ekberg's husband, who had spent a lot of time around the set, contracted scarlet fever. It didn't infect the rest of the crew, fortunately, but then the movie didn't infect the public with great enthusiasm either.

In early 1958, the 'Cold War' was in full force. Things warmed up slightly, however, when it was announced that President Eisenhower and Soviet Premier Kruschev had agreed to a summit meeting, and a full thaw followed word that Bob Hope would film a special in Russia.

Hope had had the idea for a long time, but it also took a long time to work it out. After lots of 'Red' tape, he finally arrived in Moscow on 16 March 1958 with a six-day visa. Various locations around Moscow were filmed, as well as the circus and ballerinas and ethnic dancing. Bob even got in a fashion show at the big GUM department store. When he performed his monologue to an audience of Britons and Americans it was filmed by Soviet cameramen. The film was processed in a Moscow laboratory, and before returning it Soviet officials told Bob they would appreciate it if a number of jokes were left out. They particularly objected to his reference to the space satellite Sputnik. (The Soviet Union was ahead of the US in space exploration at the time.)

The officials agreed to return the film to Hope if he would accept their deletions and pay $1,200 in lab fees. Despite the censorship, when the film was shown on NBC it was awarded the prestigious Peabody and Sylvania awards.

Ever a staunch American, Hope revealed some of his own feelings about world politics during the show's closing sequence. As he walked through the streets of Moscow, he spoke about the ever-increasing arms build-up and expressed his fervent hope for peaceful co-existence. The TV special led to Hope's next book, *I Owe Russia $1,200*.

Throughout 1958, Bob's publicity agent Mack Millar kept up a steady campaign to have Bob awarded a special honour. Bob's military shows, often at Christmas in out-of-the-way locations, had become a tradition over many years. He had received almost every conceivable award for doing them, but Millar wanted him to receive the most prestigious one that America offered, the Congressional Medal of Honour. Although he had pulled every string he could think of, and despite the many influential friends Bob had made, he had been unable to pull it off as the year ended.

In 1959, Bob was finally forced to slow down. The 1958 season had been his last on radio, although he was still performing frequently on both sides of the Atlantic, as well as doing his monthly television show, making cameo appearances in movies, and producing his own feature length western spoof, *Alias Jesse James*, with Rhonda Fleming.

His health finally succumbed to his hectic schedule. Bob

developed high blood pressure and a very serious eye problem. A blood clot in the cornea was blamed on overwork and he was forced to cancel everything but his television shows for a few months and settle down with Dolores for a rest.

Slowing down was not easy for him. He didn't really know how to rest, how to conserve energy, but Dolores made sure that he did, screening his calls, limiting his social engagements, and making sure he got eight hours sleep every night. One benefit of the new regime was that they got to spend a lot more time together.

By Christmas of that year, though, Hope was chomping at the bit. He agreed to return to do another USO tour in Alaska. He brought along the beautiful and incredibly well-endowed Jayne Mansfield, as well as the movies' new Western star, Steve McQueen, and his wife. Bob made it through the tour, but experienced some bouts of dizziness.

In 1960, Hope made just one picture, *The Facts of Life*. He was again teamed up with Lucille Ball, and Bob and Lucy were as funny together as before.

There was also the opportunity to meet a new American President, John F. Kennedy. There were jokes galore from Bob, though as usual they were basically tame; JFK and Hope got along well.

Bob's next film was a domestic comedy called *Bachelor in Paradise*. His co-star, the renowned Lana Turner, was not a good match for him and the film suffered.

The love interest from the *Road* pictures, Dorothy Lamour, was now living in semi-retirement as a wife and mother in Baltimore. A new *Road* picture was proposed, but Bing and the producers wanted a younger leading lady. Joan Collins, now famous for her TV role in *Dynasty*, was given the lead. Lamour was offered a small supporting role, humiliating her. This was the seventh of the *Road* pictures and all had been made with the famous threesome before. Even more galling was the double standard that branded her too old when she was in fact ten years younger than either Bing or Bob. She finally agreed to do the small part, partly because of the support showed her by Bob and the press. The film, made in England, was called *The Road to Hong Kong*. It was the last of the series, and probably the weakest. The highlights were cameos by Peter Sellers, Frank Sinatra, Dean Martin, David Niven and Zsa Zsa Gabor.

Hope still found it hard to take things as easy as he should have done to cure his eye problem. In 1961, he did a military tour of Newfoundland, Labrador and Greenland with Jayne Mansfield, Anita Ekberg and Dorothy Provine. He continued a heavy schedule of benefit performances as well as his monthly TV specials.

The next year saw Hope in the Washington, DC, area for some special events. His son, Tony, graduated from Georgetown University, which decided to award Papa Hope a degree at the same time. He was given an honorary doctorate in humane letters, the first of many honorary degrees he would receive.

Also in 1962, he came out with another book, *I Owe Russia $1,200*, and filmed *Call Me Bwana* with Anita Ekberg. Bob's golfing buddy, Arnold Palmer, made a brief appearance in the movie.

There were dark moments as well in 1962. That summer, Bob felt strongly the loss of his brother, Jack, to acute hepatitis. Shortly thereafter one of his writers succumbed to a heart attack and then Mack Millar, the indefatigable publicist who had spent the last months of his life working on getting Bob the Congressional Medal of Honour, also died suddenly of a heart attack. Millar had reached his goal, however: Hope was finally going to receive the medal.

After another Command Performance in London, Hope planned a Christmas tour of the Far East. On his itinerary were Japan, Korea, Okinawa, Taiwan, the Philippines and Guam. In addition, he had secretly worked a deal with the military to travel into South Vietnam while he was near that country.

However, it was not to be. He was not allowed into the country because the Defense Department had decided that it was too risky. Nonetheless, the show was memorable. Hope taped it for subsequent showing on NBC. He had brought along Lana Turner, Janis Paige and Anita Bryant. When it was aired, it was nominated for an Emmy Award and won a Golden Globe and a *TV Guide* award.

On 11 September 1963, Mack Millar's dream came true. With his family in attendance, Hope received the $2,500 Congressional Medal of Honour from President Kennedy in the Oval Office at the White House.

It seems that all the strong publicity and public relations representing Bob as an All-American Booster began to be believed by Hope himself. Bob began planning a Bob Hope Museum within a month of receiving the Congressional Medal, and revealed that he had donated funds for a Bob Hope Theatre at Southern Methodist University in Dallas, Texas.

In the autumn of 1963, Bob was again plagued by his eye problem. It grew worse and several doctors were consulted on both coasts. During this period of frustration, Bob joined with the nation in mourning the loss of its youngest president, John Fitzgerald Kennedy, who was the victim of an assassin's bullet in Texas.

In December, Bob's eyes received their second photocoagulation treatment, a delicate procedure designed to stop the haemorrhaging going on behind his eyes. He was forced to wear dark glasses with small holes in them directing his vision.

Bob was due to leave on another USO Christmas tour of Europe, but everyone thought he would call it off. Hope refused. Although his ego was great, his sense of responsibility was stronger. The Defense Department sent along one of its best medicos and Hope joined his troupe in Ankara, Turkey, after a short rest. Despite feeling weak and woozy, Hope found that the lights and the audience worked their usual magic on him. He felt rejuvenated. Applause, he felt, was his best therapy, an appreciative audience his best medicine, and he spent far more time on stage than anyone expected.

Hope felt so good after ten days of entertaining that in his last show in Naples he actually did a challenge dance with an old vaudevillian he had brought along.

January of 1964 marked the beginning of what was to be one of the most difficult times in Hope's long career. The nation's politics were becoming increasingly liberal. Although the 1950s had been a decade of life-as-the-powerful-might-like-it, emotions began to stir in those segments of the population which were disadvantaged in an essentially white and male-oriented culture. Blacks marched and insisted on constitutional rights that had frequently been denied them, foreshadowing the passage of a landmark Civil Rights Act in 1964, and women asked why careers and influence in government and industry were denied them. The US military involvement in Vietnam was growing rapidly, though as in Korea, the United States had never formally declared war in the imbroglio. Despite the lack of a declaration, however, America's sons were killing and being killed.

Americans began to learn about things that had been going on behind their backs, such as assassinations by the CIA and blacklists and wiretapping by the FBI. Rock and folk musicians were stirring up the young generation, who were already moving toward a cultural revolution. All facets of society were to be examined, from sexual mores to religious beliefs, politics and the role of authority. Even the Catholic Church was being liberalized in the wake of Vatican II.

An American institution such as Bob Hope was bound to come under fire as people began to question established values and ask if they were being told the truth. Was he part of what many felt was a plot by the government to deceive its citizens? Although it would be some time before major changes would be made, this spirit of questioning meant that Bob Hope, although really a minor player in the scheme of things, would become a focal point of society's scrutiny.

Radicals by no means made up a majority in society, although they were frequently the most noticeable and vocal. Many people in the 1960s continued to live and think as they had in the 1950s, and Hope maintained his popularity with them. His two younger children, Nora and Kelly, gave him 'inside information', and he made a point of courting the younger audience. He toured many colleges and universities, continuing to draw large enthusiastic crowds.

Hope's only movie of 1964 displayed his interest in catering to the youth audience. In this film, called *I'll Take Sweden*, Bob plays the protective father of Tuesday Weld, who is in love with the motorcycle-riding Frankie Avalon. The movie was directed by Freddie DeCordova, best known for directing Ronald Reagan in *Bedtime for Bonzo* and for his long association with Johnny Carson on the *Tonight Show*. Frankie Avalon had made it big as a singer and as the star of a series of 'Bikini' movies with Annette Funicello, such as *Beach Party*, *Bikini Beach*, *Muscle Beach Party*, and *Beach Blanket Bingo*.

Hope's movie was a nice try, but it didn't really work. Critic Leonard Maltin saw in it only 'witless proceedings, lacking usual Hope humour'.

At Christmas 1964 Hope's USO tour was on the road to Vietnam. It was his twenty-first year of entertaining the troops. This trip, though, was kept secret for security reasons. The Defense Department did not want any of the large audiences that gathered to be targets for enemy action.

Along with seasoned troupers Anita Bryant and Janis Paige, Hope brought a new young star, Jill St. John, as well as his son, Tony, who was on vacation from Harvard Law School, and Anna Maria Alberghetti. Counting the musicians, technicians and performers, Hope travelled with a crew of 75 people. Before arriving in Vietnam, the crew made their way through Korea, Okinawa and Thailand. In Bangkok, they were treated to a dinner with the King and Queen at the Royal Palace.

In Vietnam they began what was code-named Operation Big Cheer. They travelled through great danger to perform and were rewarded with huge audiences. The tour took them over 23,000 miles and was an adventure in itself. Naturally, it was filmed for television. After a publicity blitz, the special was seen in more than half of American households when it aired. Focusing on the soldiers and the conditions in which they lived and fought, it brought in Hope's largest TV audience to date.

Chrysler now became Bob's sponsor. In order to exploit their new star, Chrysler decided to involve Hope in the Palm Springs Classic, a charity golf tournament Hope had participated in many times in the past. Renamed the Bob Hope Desert Classic, it became a rival to Bing Crosby's tournament at Pebble Beach.

The Classic became one of golf's most prestigious events, gathering together famous pros like Arnie Palmer, Jack Nicklaus and Gary Player, in addition to celebrities like Andy Williams, Frank Sinatra, Lawrence Welk and Danny Thomas. They were joined by socialites like Walter Annenberg (the owner of *TV Guide*, among other things), Leonard Firestone of automotive fame and Hope's old pal, Dwight Eisenhower.

After the tournament, Hope decided to do another TV special about his trip to Vietnam. He had a lot of unused footage and felt it his duty to show the American people how important the role of the GI was in the anti-communist 'war'. Chrysler was somewhat sceptical, as boys had already started burning their draft cards and anti-war demonstrations had begun. Bob and his golfing partner, ex-General and ex-President 'Ike' Eisenhower, though, were in agreement. Because most of Hope's cronies were members of the 'Establishment', it is easy to see how his political opinions were influenced toward the right. His genuine regard for America's fighting men, however, was as important to Bob as his political beliefs. He felt strongly that they were fighting for a just case. If they were being injured and dying, he felt that it had to be for a good reason; he could not allow himself to think otherwise.

Bob continued to rake in awards during 1964. He received his fourth and fifth honorary doctorate degrees, the latter in the company of fellow honoree Richard M. Nixon. He was awarded the first annual Screen Actors Guild honour 'for outstanding achievement in fostering the finest ideals of the acting profession', as well as the Splendid American Award from the Tom Dooley Foundation, an NBC affiliates' award and numerous others.

Early in 1965, Hope got his caricature on the cover of *TV Guide*. Inside was an article which, while generally positive, carried the most critical description of him that ever appeared in a national magazine. The article said:

> He is . . . a socio-political force. As such he belongs to no one, not even himself . . . In the 25 years since old Ski-Nose first rose to fame on the coattails of Bing Crosby . . . he has raised close to a quarter of a million dollars for worthy causes. He has travelled to almost every country in the world, often to entertain troops at Christmas . . . His stature as the world's foremost funny humanitarian has put in his pocket more brass hats, politicos, industrial wheel horses and Russian generals than any comedian since Will Rogers, and has widened his sphere of influence-without-portfolio to the point where he is sometimes called upon to facilitate matters which have baffled the State Department.[1]

He carried on his charity work, establishing a halfway house for delinquent boys in Cincinnati called The Bob Hope House, which he continued to support. He also did a military tour during that summer in the Dominican Republic, where President Johnson had stationed troops to avert a Communist takeover.

Bob made his fifty-first movie, *Boy, Did I Get a Wrong Number!* with Elke Sommer and Phyllis Diller, but his movie career was no longer exactly thriving, and this latest effort was not particularly well received.

Hope returned to Southeast Asia for Christmas of 1965 and film footage of his tour shown on national television added to the massive coverage of the war on the nightly news. Although he was not regarded so much as a hero by the public as he had been in previous wars, the architects of the war in Vietnam depended on his support. The Senate Foreign Relations Committee was holding hearings on the war that were frequently critical of the Administration's actions and position. A good-sized segment of the population was openly opposed to the war. To the White House, Hope's actions were a breath of fresh air.

Hope was guest of honour at the USO's twenty-fifth anniversary celebration, and was awarded its silver medal by President Lyndon Johnson, whose jokes were appreciated by the audience as much as Hope's.

In April, construction began on the Eisenhower Medical Center in the Palm Springs area on land donated by the Hopes. Dolores eventually chaired its board of directors and remains extremely active in its fundraising. The Center's principal mission is the study and treatment of respiratory and heart diseases.

It was at this time that American politics took one of its odd turns. Bob Hope was approached to consider running for President. Since it would have been impossible, because Bob was not born in the United States, those who suggested it actually considered introducing a Bill in Congress to override that rule. In the past he had been asked to run for senator from California, although nothing ever came of it.

Hope's enduring popularity was part of the reasoning behind this unique offer. What Richard Nixon later called the 'Silent Majority' was still firmly on Bob's side. The draw of his TV shows and the respect of cheering audiences at his performances, as well as that of many important people, kept Hope from realizing that another group of Americans, growing every day, did not agree about the danger of the Communist threat in a little country thousands of miles away. Although Bob hated the fact that in Vietnam Americans were dying, he never questioned whether or not it was for a righteous cause.

Bob's album released at this time, *On the Road to Vietnam*, received criticism for seeming 'opportunistic'. He also published his latest book, with the eccentric title *Five Women I Love: Bob Hope's Vietnam Story*.

His 1966 Southeast Asia tour included Phyllis Diller, Anita Bryant, Joey Heatherton and Vic Damone. His family also came along, and Dolores took the stage to sing 'White Christmas'. He chatted frequently during that trip with General Westmoreland, who reinforced Bob's feelings about the war. Nearly three months after he returned home, intelligence reports indicated that Hope had been the object of a failed assassination attempt while in Vietnam.

At Christmas, 1967, Bob was again in Vietnam, and at this time was featured on the cover of *Time*. It was a generally favourable article. A week after his return, the 77-day Tet Offensive was begun by the North Vietnamese and the war entered its bloodiest phase. On 13 May 1968, the Paris Peace Talks began and Hope received the Sylvanus Thayer Award* at West Point.

Between these events Bob made another movie, *Eight on the Lam*, co-starring Phyllis Diller, Jonathan Winters and Jill St. John. Leonard Maltin has said of the film, 'Another of Hope's horrible 60s comedies casts him as a widower with seven children who finds $10,000; even Winters can't help this dud. Rated: BOMB.'[2]

Hope's next film was *The Private Navy of Sgt. O'Farrell*, which met with even less success. This one again starred Phyllis Diller, along with Gina Lollobrigida. Maltin has been no kinder about this film: 'Of the many terrible Hope comedies of the 1960s, this may be the worst. Unfunny and even offensive. Rated: BOMB.'[3]

Hope went back to Vietnam again for Christmas, 1968. That year was remarkable for, among other things, one of the most heated and violent presidential campaigns in American history. Richard Nixon was elected President over Hubert Humphrey and George Wallace. The Democratic Convention in Mayor Daley's Chicago was the focus of a bloody riot in which police were seen using brutal force against the nation's increasingly radical students. Even mainstream America – Nixon's 'Silent Majority' – began to wonder about the continued conflict in Vietnam as they watched nightly television images of brutal

* Named after the founder of West Point, the Sylvanus Thayer Award is given by the US Military Academy Association of Graduates to the American citizen whose services to his country best exemplify the West Point motto: 'Duty, Honour, Country'.

fighting and huge casualties. Hope's Christmas tours were also broadcast, showing America the faces of its young fighting men who had seen and endured too much. The draft took the poor and uneducated, blacks, farm kids, and the disenfranchised, but middle-class boys finagled student deferments or left for Canada and Europe.

The big news for Bob Hope in 1968 was the wedding of his daughter Linda. An enormous party was held and among the 1,000 guests were Vice-President Elect Spiro Agnew, California Governor and Mrs Ronald Reagan, Ohio Governor Jim Rhodes, Senator George Murphy, Generals Jimmy Doolittle and Omar Bradley, Cardinal McIntyre, Ed Sullivan, Earl Wilson, and Hollywood's Danny Kaye, Gregory Peck, Jack Benny, Danny Thomas, Loretta Young, Irene Dunne, and of course Dorothy Lamour and Bing Crosby.

Spiro Agnew and Hope had been friends for about a year. They met at one of Hope's award ceremonies and quickly became golfing buddies. In fact, Hope's gagwriters provided a lot of the material Agnew used in his speeches, including later gibes at the press and television.

Hope grew more political as his personal life became increasingly populated by important politicians. He began taking part in Republican Party fund-raising activities. His life continued apace with golf, additional honorary degrees, the Christmas tour of Vietnam and, sadly, more eye problems. Bob was forced to take vacations and rest from time to time as the problem would flare up.

Hope's next movie was *How to Commit Marriage* with Jane Wyman and Jackie Gleason. The movie attempted to be 'mod', but what was touted as new was already old. Mel Brooks and Woody Allen were making movies at the same time which made Hope's suffer horribly by comparison.

Bob and Dolores also experienced a number of painful losses. Their friend Dwight Eisenhower passed away, and then Bob's brother Ivor, his partner in Hope Metal Products. Less than a week later his brother George died of throat cancer.

By all evidence Hope was in a low period. He continued to have health problems, he lost people he loved, his movies were 'bombs', and he was the target of serious criticism. But he wasn't named Hope for nothing.

Bob continued to win popularity polls. Not only the power brokers loved him, but the majority of American citizens as well. His TV specials continued to garner high ratings; and audiences, including those at colleges and universities, flocked to see him in person. The soldiers, sailors and marines whom he entertained saw him as an influential friend on their side and a welcome touch of home. Feeling a responsibility to his audience, as well as a need for their cheers and applause, allowed Bob to overcome his physical problems and come alive anytime he found himself on a stage.

8

Politics and Plaudits

By October 1969, the United States was mourning not only the loss of its young men in Southeast Asia, but the sharp division of the citizenry at home as well. Campus unrest was high, fuelled primarily by a dismay over what was called an immoral war. Students and other young people marched and demonstrated, eventually drawing out sympathetic feelings in others, even members of government. Bob's friend Stuart Symington was one of those who joined that point of view, to Hope's dismay. The truly American, it seems, required an additional label: 'Hawk' or 'Dove'.

In their protest against the war, the doves, at first predominantly university students and older intellectuals and radicals, gained the support of many church leaders, university presidents, celebrities, and prominent government figures. The single message of the protest was to get out of Vietnam *now*.

Hope refused to take the anti-war movement seriously. Along with President Nixon, he believed that America could not afford to 'lose' a war. It never had before, as long as one conveniently ignored the Korean conflict. To Hope it seemed dishonourable to withdraw without a victory. He never considered that it might have been dishonourable to be involved in the first place.

Nixon made his 'silent majority' speech, in which he asked for public approval of his plan to withdraw troops on his own secret schedule. The White House received a flurry of positive telegrams after the speech, although many believed that the messages were orchestrated by Republican party leaders.

To counter the anti-war movement, the Administration planned a 'National Unity Week' for November 1969 along with the American Legion, Veterans of Foreign Wars, and others. The ploy was to dilute the effect of a large anti-war demonstration scheduled for the same time in Washington. Hope, asked to be national chairman, agreed.

In the meantime, he continued his successful series of college appearances. On 15 November, the day of the big Washington protest, Hope was performing in Seattle at the University of Washington. Outside there were picket lines, and seven hundred protesters held a candlelight vigil.

Hope frequently protested that politically he was middle-of-the-road, though his outspoken defence of Agnew and Nixon indicated that he was partisan. There was nothing unusual, though, in an entertainer having political convictions and being outspoken about them. Jane Fonda, Shirley MacLaine, Charlton Heston and other well-known entertainers have spoken out for political candidates in recent years.

In 1969, Hope showed his support of US troops by planning a worldwide tour of military installations. Starting with a White House celebration that included the Nixons, the Agnews, General Westmoreland, members of the Cabinet, congressmen and other notables, the group set off from Andrews Air Force Base. Bob's eye problem was bothering him, but he went on regardless. The first stop was Berlin, followed by Rome, Turkey, Bangkok and then Vietnam.

Because of massive advance publicity, the international news corps followed Hope's tour. They were there to record the boos of the GIs when Hope announced that Nixon had a peace plan. Hope mistook the peace sign many held up as the World War II 'V for Victory' sign. When the film of the tour was broadcast on NBC in January 1970, it broke the Nielsen ratings record.

In 1970, Hope worked hard collecting the money required to complete the Eisenhower Medical Center. His plan for a $1,000 a plate dinner (for which he picked up the tab for expenses) brought in $1.5 million of the $7 million needed. NBC broadcast the event, calling it 'Five Stars for a Five-Star Man' with Bing Crosby, Raquel Welch, Johnny Cash, Ray Bolger and Hope. Honorary chairmen of the dinner were Nixon, Johnson and Truman, and industrial giants that attended gave generously.

Critics later noted that among the guests at the star-studded gala there was not one black face. Hope replied that he had invited two blacks, but neither could make it.

Hope's efforts having been successful, the dedication of the hospital took place in 1971. Nixon, Agnew and Reagan attended.

Besides raising funds for the Medical Centre, in 1970 Hope also did a benefit for the Ed White youth centre, named after one of the astronaut casualties from the Apollo fire. Nearly filling the 50,000 seat Houston Astrodome, Bob entertained the crowd along with Gregory Peck, Cary Grant, David Janssen, Dorothy Lamour, Joey Heatherton, Glen Campbell, Robert Goulet, Frankie Valli and the Four Seasons, and O. J. Simpson.

Believing that he was helping bring the country together, Hope chose 4 July 1970 as a day to rally against the nation's peace dissenters. Called Honour America Day, it was set in Washington. Bob partnered himself with the evangelist Billy Graham. In addition to religious ceremonies, there were fireworks and entertainment planned, designed and staged by Walt Disney Productions.

On 9 June 1970, the *Washington Post* expressed the concerns of many who questioned the wisdom of reinforcing patriotism with Walt Disney and movieland fantasy. The paper said:

> The suspicion, as we get it, is that any effort to make something different out of this year's Fourth of July observances is going to take on the trappings of a pro-war rally in support of President Nixon's Vietnam policy, no matter how much the sponsors may wish to avoid it, just by the identity of the principal figures who have so far associated themselves with the ideal . . . It needs a broader mix, not just of Democrats as well as Republicans but of dissenters as well as supporters . . . They could make the point a little more explicit by trying to engage the active support of responsible leaders on the other side of the great national debates – of Hubert Humphrey, to take one example, or George McGovern.

The critics' voices were heard, and Humphrey, McGovern, and Senators Muskie and Mansfield all joined in. The entertainers included Jack Benny, Dinah Shore, Kate Smith, Red Skelton, Roberta Flack, Dorothy Lamour, Pat Boone, Barbara Eden, the New Christy Minstrels, the Golddiggers, Connie Stevens, the Young Americans and Fred Waring. With the possible exception of Miss Flack, though, this group was hardly designed to appeal to young people. To use an expression of the time, it was a 'white bread' cast of has-beens. The executive chairman was the ultra-conservative Mormon hotelier, Willard Marriot. He and Hope reckoned that the event would be bigger than Woodstock.

Early events of the day were not what the organizers had hoped for. Protesters and demonstrators were out in force, conspicuously being rounded up by the police. Adding insult to injury, it rained. The rain stopped by the time Hope took the stage for his three-hour spectacular, but the demonstrations grew louder and more angry. Street vendors' carts were dumped into the Reflecting Pool and bottles were thrown. The hecklers, fenced off from the 'regular' audience, threw tear gas canisters over the fence. The situation grew so bad that Hope needed a police escort to leave the area.

Hope continued to campaign for Republican candidates and help in fund-raising for Nixon and Agnew.* With Hope's campaigning came a greater outcry that Hope was exploiting his celebrity status to deliver political messages. Despite his constitutionally-guaranteed right to freedom of speech, critics claimed that Hope had undue advantage due to the image that he had built up for himself over the years with the help of his supporters. His army of publicists had succeeded in convincing large segments of the population that he was as much a symbol of America as Mom and apple pie. He was thought to be a real patriot, and patriot he was.

Bob Hope attracted attention because what he said was opinion-leading. His opinions reinforced what the nation had learned in the nationalistic days of a world war and in the reconstruction following that war, and reflected the ideals that were taught in the churches and the schools. The country was going through an enormous social change, a frightening thing to many because it involves the unknown. Questions arose: What will replace that which is done away with? In the world of 'free love' what happens to the family? In a world where authority is challenged, who will lead? If Communism isn't evil, then what about capitalism? Hope said that everything Americans had been brought up to believe was right and didn't need to be changed. Certain precepts were worth espousing: life should stay the way it was; respect authority and believe what your govern-

* Dolores' nephew, Peter Malatesta, was an Agnew aide.

ment tells you. Aim for the idealized, stereotypical life, despite any problems it may bring. Problems you know are better than the problems you don't know. These views made Bob Hope popular with a lot of people.

In a *Reader's Digest* poll of 250,000 high school students, Hope topped the list in popularity in the US, finishing second only to the Beatles world-wide. Political scientists, interestingly enough, found that there was a solid portion of the public who would support a president no matter who he was or what he had done simply because he was the president. It seems that Hope, too, fell into this category of unquestioning, blind acceptance of authority.

Journalists wrote that Hope was no longer as popular with the GIs as he had been. His tours of the military were called publicity gimmicks, for his own benefit as well as for the Administration and the Pentagon. Bob found such statements hard to believe based on the reception he received when entertaining the soldiers.

In March 1971, the New York City Council of Churches planned to give Hope their Family of Man Award. They were persuaded to withdraw his name. Disturbed, angry and annoyed at this rejection and all the criticism he was receiving, Hope was genuinely baffled. He had maintained on several occasions that war itself was bad but sometimes there were no alternatives. He was unable to reconcile the protestors' attitudes with the obvious affection he received from his audiences as well as his high ratings on television and his popularity in the polls.

In December, 1971, Hope was in Vietnam again, this time with a secret mission. Determined to tackle a problem that had disturbed him for a long time, he was going to try to get the POWs released. Working with various US Ambassadors and the CIA, he met with the North Vietnamese at their embassy in Vientiane, later requesting a visa to go to North Vietnam and negotiate directly. In Hope's meetings there with the First Secretary, the two men discussed an exchange of money for the prisoners, with the funds targeted for Vietnamese children.

Once back home, Hope travelled to Washington four times to meet with Nixon, Kissinger and Rogers. The Administration, he learned, was continuing its own negotiations and everything possible was being done. Nixon has always maintained, as does Hope, that Hope met with the North Vietnamese on his own initiative with the subsequent approval of the President. As in the past, though, he had been assisted by the CIA and the Foreign Service.

By this time, Nixon had made his historic trips to both the Soviet Union and China with the assistance of Henry Kissinger. The war seemed to be winding down, prompting Hope to talk about not making any more trips to Vietnam. Now nearing 70 years old, Bob campaigned for Nixon's re-election in 1972. The first news of the Watergate scandal started to break that year, although it would never be conclusively proved how far into the White House the problem went.

In 1972 Bob also made his last movie for cinema showing, *Cancel My Reservation*, but it was no better than the films he made in the 1960s. He also began working with a writer on another new book, a retrospective of his 40-year career in the movies. It was to be called *The Last Christmas Show*.

Christmas, 1972 was in fact the date of Bob Hope's last Vietnam Christmas show. Because Bob announced that this would be his last Christmas show, he received awards everywhere he went. Dolores came along and again sang 'White Christmas' in the show.

Not long after their return, just two days before the TV special was aired, Nixon suspended bombing in Vietnam and deactivated the mines.

Before long, America was embroiled in one of its most serious domestic crises: Watergate. Hope, although saddened by the revelations of cynicism and corruption, never gave up his friendship with either Agnew or Nixon.

Following his seventieth birthday in 1973, Hope continued to fill his schedule with awards and honours, road trips, stage performances, TV shows and benefits, and of course, golf.

He signed up with an exclusive sponsor for his TV shows, this time Texaco. His original contract with them called for seven hours of programming per year for three years at $3,150,000 per year, plus another $250,000 to do commercials.

Texaco asked Hope to freshen up his act, requesting that he get an entirely new staff. He did so. Sadly enough, his employees heard about being replaced not from him, but through the rumour mill. He replaced everyone, including Mort Lachman, who had been with him for 28 years, Lester White, who had been with him since vaudeville, and Norman Sullivan, who had worked with Bob since the Pepsodent radio show.

When he was 72, Bob received a singular honour – an honorary high school diploma. Hope had been awarded 32 honorary advanced degrees, but he had never got his own high school diploma. The honorary one commemorated his patronage of The Bob Hope High School for Crippled Children, the first of its kind, in Port Arthur, Texas.

Three days before the 1976 American Bicentennial Celebration, ex-Briton Bob Hope received one of the three awards he holds most dear, the title Commander of the British Empire (CBE). (The other two awards are the Congressional Medal of Honor and West Point's Sylvanus Thayer Award.) Queen Elizabeth awarded him the medal at the British embassy in Washington, along with Walter Annenberg, Eugene Ormandy, and Wallace Sterling, the chancellor of Stanford University.

The next day, Bob introduced President Gerald Ford at the Kennedy Center celebration. President Ford had left an Air Force jet at Hope's disposal to get him there.

Not long afterward, plans were under way to shoot one more *Road* picture. Crosby, Hope and Lamour would play themselves in locations ranging from London to Saudi Arabia to Moscow. It was to be called *The Road to Tomorrow*.

In the meantime, Crosby was getting ready to celebrate his 50 years in show business with a huge gala televised from Pasadena. Crosby's two guest stars were Hope and Pearl Bailey. At the end of the show, when Hope and Bailey were back in their dressing rooms, Bing tripped as he was leaving the stage and fell into the orchestra pit. He hurt himself so badly that plans for the film had to be postponed.

Hope filled his time with golf and benefits, often combining the two. He made guest appearances on a number of television shows, picked up honorary degrees thirty-seven through forty, and published his seventh book, *The Road to Hollywood*, co-authored with Bob Thomas.

On 14 October 1977, Hope was called and told that Bing had suffered a heart attack on the golf course and was dead. Hope did something he had rarely done in his career: he cancelled his scheduled stage appearances the next two nights and retired to his home.

The funeral was on 18 October. Bob and Dolores were among

the thirty people attending the private service. Bing had left specific instructions that only those closest to him should attend his funeral. Hope had been specifically mentioned in Crosby's will as one of those people he wanted to come.

Bob revamped his planned TV special ten days later and called it 'On the Road with Bing'.

Hope and Crosby had been closely linked in the public mind. Therefore, when Hope turned 75 the next year he received an enormous outpouring of affection and honour. Although Bob was not even close to dying, people wanted to make certain he knew how they felt about him before they lost him as well.

So far Hope was not even slowing down. In 1978 alone, 'Rapid Robert' gave 131 stage shows, appeared on 30 TV programmes, picked up his forty-second honorary degree, putted in 25 charity golf games and logged over 250,000 miles.[1] He was still going strong.

One of those TV appearances was in April, when Hope was the sole Master of Ceremonies for the Academy Award presentations. It was Oscar's fiftieth anniversary and a huge celebration was planned. It was both an honour and somehow natural for Bob to be in the centre of things. (Strangely, the most memorable moment of the ceremony turned out to be Vanessa Redgrave's denunciation of Zionism as she accepted the award for Best Supporting Actress for her role in *Julia*.)

Predictably, the USO also wished to honour Hope on his seventy-fifth birthday. Hope agreed on condition that the celebration would benefit the USO building fund. The USO was planning to build its World Headquarters in Washington, which would be named 'The Bob Hope USO Center' and was to include Bob's long-desired museum of memorabilia of his own life and career.

NBC and Texaco also got in on the act. Hope's role called for him to relax and let some other big-time entertainers salute him at a televised black-tie affair at the Kennedy Center. The event turned out to be only the first annual TV birthday party for Hope. His birthday, 30 May, on the threshold of Memorial Day weekend, occurs during the Neilsen 'sweeps', a period when viewership ratings are heavily scrutinized and the networks trot out their best in a highly competitive 'ratings war'. Hope's special served as a sure-fire winner for NBC.

The 1978 show included Pearl Bailey, Lucille Ball, George Burns, Sammy Davis, Jr., Redd Foxx, Elliott Gould, Alan King, Dorothy Lamour, Carol Lawrence, Fred MacMurray, the Muppets, Donny and Marie Osmond, Telly Savalas, George C. Scott, Elizabeth Taylor, Danny Thomas, John Wayne, and, of course, Kathryn Crosby and Dolores Hope. Dolores began a tradition of singing to her husband on the show.

Shortly before the show, Hope attended a reception at the White House hosted by Jimmy Carter. Bob also hosted a party himself and was a guest of honour at a luncheon held by congressmen's wives, as well as being the object of an incredibly unconventional hour of speeches on the floor of the House of Representatives.

Despite the early hour (for Hope at least), Bob roused himself by 10:00 a.m. and joined his family in the House of Representatives gallery. He expected to hear a resolution passed honouring him for his humanitarian work, but this in no way prepared him for what actually happened. One by one, the Representatives spoke of the value of Hope's humour and his concern for charitable service. When Ohio Congresswoman Oakar took the floor, she praised him for his support of the Cleveland Indians baseball team, which Hope owns. New York's Wydler said, 'I am going to violate the House rules and address a comment to our distinguished guest'.

Speaker Tip O'Neill broke in. 'The gentleman is aware of the rules?'

Wydler said he was and continued, 'On behalf of the people in my district, Bob, and of the people of America, just this one sentence sums up our feelings toward you, and that is, "Thanks for the memories"'. The House applauded.

The next speaker was Congressman Moakley of Massachusetts, who noted that it was against the rules to sing in the House, but proceeded to recite:

> Thanks for the memories
> Of golf with Tip and Ford,
> None of us ignored,
> It sure took guts to sink those putts
> Which showed how well you scored
> How lovely it was.

Bob with his first real stage partner, Lloyd 'Lefty' Durbin, in Cleveland.
Culver Pictures, Inc.

The Hope family in Cleveland: *(from left to right)* Jack, George, Harry (father), Ivor, Jim, Sid, Avis (mother), Bob, Fred. *Culver Pictures, Inc.*

With Charles Butterworth in *Thanks for the Memory* (1938). *Culver Pictures, Inc.*

Crazy golfers: Bob and Bing fooling around on the fairway.
Movie Star News

Bob entertaining USAAF personnel on an American airfield in Britain in 1943. *AP/Wide World Photos*

Crosby and Hope in *Road to Morocco* (1942). *Movie Tone News*

Bing Crosby, Bob Hope, Dorothy Lamour – and friend – in *Road to Rio* (1947). *MovieTone News*

Bob looks quizzically at his fourth Special Oscar, awarded in 1965.
Culver Pictures, Inc.

From left to right: President Reagan, Dolores Hope, Nancy Reagan, Bob Hope, former President Gerald Ford. Dwight Eisenhower, Hope's first presidential golfing partner, looks on. *AP/Wide World Photos*

Bob chats with the Queen before the Silver Jubilee Royal Variety Gala at the London Palladium on 22 November, 1977. *AP/Wide World Photos*

Bob entertaining sailors and marines aboard the battleship
USS *New Jersey* stationed off the coast of Beirut on Christmas Eve, 1983.
AP/Wide World Photos

With the Republicans at the White House you've feasted
With the Democrats at the White House you fasted,
Now Carter's here
Serving Billy Beer

And thanks for the memories
Of road trips that were fun
That kept Bing on the run,
We're very glad you got to make
The road to Washington
We thank you so much.

Nine more Representatives spoke kudos, followed by the
Minority Whip, Robert Michel, who went ahead and broke the
rules against singing:

Thanks for the memories,
Of places you have gone
To cheer our soldiers on,
The President sent Kissinger
But you sent Jill St. John
We thank you so much!

Seventy plus five is now your age, Bob
We're glad to see you still upon the stage, Bob,
We hope you make a decent living wage, Bob,
For the more you make –
The more we take!

The last to speak was the Speaker himself. He said:

I explain to our guests, particularly, that singing in the
House, and speaking in a foreign language, are not
customary in the House.
    Also, you may be interested to know that in my 25 years in
Congress, and I know there are members senior to me here,
never before have I ever witnessed anything of this nature.
    The rules say that nobody can be introduced from the
gallery, and that rule cannot be waived. Presidents' wives
and former Presidents merely sit there. I have seen
distinguished visitors, who have come to the House, sit in

the galleries, but never before have I seen anything
compared to what is transpiring on the floor today.

It is a show of appreciation, of love and affection to a
great American, and I think it is a beautiful tribute.

When O'Neill finished with the words 'Happy Birthday, Bob
Hope', the House got to its feet, sang Happy Birthday and
applauded for a long time. Tears came to Hope's eyes as he stood
before them, alongside his wife and children. It was a great
moment.

A year later, the renowned Film Society of Lincoln Center in
New York decided to honour Hope's movie career. The decision
stemmed from a televised interview of Woody Allen by Dick
Cavett, in which Allen revealed how much respect he had for
Hope's screen comedy. He mentioned that it would be fun to edit
together scenes from various Hope movies showing his range
and talent. Allen was given the opportunity to do so for the
Lincoln Center.

Allen put together a 63-minute compilation using scenes from
17 movies Hope had made between 1938 and 1954. He also
narrated the piece. Called 'My Favorite Comedian', the film also
pointed out Hope's influence on his (Woody Allen's) work.

At its presentation, Cavett was the host. Woody Allen, plead-
ing fear of large audiences, let his film work speak for him.

Not everyone was impressed with the show or with Hope.
Perhaps predictably, a columnist for *The Village Voice* wrote:
Hope's wisecracks have always left me with a bad taste in my
mouth. His humour, which I'm sure he'd construe as harmless,
ridicules the underdog, thereby making the 'regular guy' feel
superior.[2]

The columnist went on to remark on the offensiveness of
Hope's gags or jokes about Native Americans, women and
homosexuality. In describing the party after the presentation, he
notes: At the reception that followed, Hope entered the party
accompanied by an aggressive cordon of guards. They escorted
him to a table as if he were Nixon at an anti-war rally.

In 1979, Hope's reputation brought him to China. China's
Ministry of Culture invited him to give a seminar on acting and
show some of the films highlighted in the Woody Allen tribute.
Hope had wanted to make the visit since Kissinger had re-

opened relations with the giant nation behind the 'Bamboo Curtain'. After six years of trying, he finally got permission and an invitation, in return for China receiving world-wide rights (after its US premiere) to the TV show Hope would film.

Bob's daughter Linda, now divorced, came to work for her father and he decided to give her this opportunity to show her stuff. She was to be the producer of the TV special.

Along with support staff, Bob and Dolores arrived in Peking (Beijing) on Saturday, 16 June 1979. Bob was unrecognized, bereft of autograph seekers or *paparazzi* with flashing cameras or Army bands or applauding crowds. No one knew who he was. During the next week he scouted locations in Peking, Shanghai, and at the Great Wall.

Soon Hope's cast arrived, a truly American mixture. Included were ballet star Mikhail Barishnikov, mimes Shields and Yarnell, country music star Crystal Gayle, soul singers Peaches and Herb and *Sesame Street* star Big Bird. The eclectic group drew interested crowds as they set up to shoot scenes before major landmarks.

The month-long visit was turned into a three-hour television special, entitled fittingly enough, 'The Road to China'.

Bob turned 77 years old in 1980 and still showed no sign of slowing up. In that year he starred in five 90-minute NBC specials, made guest appearances on 23 talk shows, appeared on six telethons, played one-man shows on 24 campuses, worked 35 banquets, and went on the road for twelve weeks in the summer.[3] Of course, the list neglects to include the benefits, the long, nightly walks, and the frequent golf games. It would be an exhausting schedule for a man half his age, but Bob seemed tireless.

In 1980, he also inaugurated the Bob Hope British Classic, another annual golf tournament whose proceeds were designed for various charities, including the Bob Hope Theatre in his native town Eltham in England.

In May 1981, Hope's seventy-eighth birthday was celebrated in a special from West Point. *Variety*, the show-biz newspaper, used the opportunity to point out Bob's popularity over the years as measured by the Nielsen ratings.

Variety reported that over the past 30 years, beginning with his 1950–1951 season, Hope had earned overall ratings with 'no serious competition in the tv (sic) field'. Of his 213 specials, 54 had garnered a 50-share or better (that is, 50+ per cent of the TV viewing audience). Four of those shows had earned whopping 70-or-more-shares.[4].

Bob's ratings, however, had slipped somewhat during the last two seasons, leading some to suspect the influence of his daughter, Linda, who had been his producer. Whether or not she was responsible for the ratings decline, she lost the job.

Variety had this to say about Hope's popularity:

> His is an unparalleled record of ratings achievement for a man of any age and none the less astonishing despite the fact that his appeal has begun to slide a bit in the past decade. That's slide, not slump – Hope is still a tough man to shave on any given day, no matter what the competition. It could be that his slippage will continue in the future, but with his track record to date – don't bet on it.[5]

That spring, Hope gave his support to two concerns. He pushed hard for handgun registration in the wake of recent assassination attempts on Ronald Reagan and Pope John Paul II. Hope also rounded up support for a benefit dinner for the USO building fund in October. Bob was particularly proud of a $500,000 donation from the government of West Germany.

It was at this time that some veterans made a stand *not* to honour Hope. Rep. Bobbi Fiedler of California had introduced a bill to name a California veterans' hospital after Hope, but was forced to drop the idea when her mail turned out to be 'overwhelmingly' against the idea. Ms Fiedler reported that main objection was that Hope was not in fact a veteran.

Also in 1981, Hope performed at a Frank Sinatra-produced gala honouring the inauguration of President Reagan. He also performed with George Burns and Johnny Carson in a TV special called 'A Love Letter to Jack Benny',

On 22 October 1981, NBC televised the opening celebration of the Gerald R. Ford Presidential Museum in Grand Rapids, Michigan. Ford and Hope were by now good friends, and Hope hosted the event.

The audience included the Reagans, the Bushes, Canada's Prime Minister Pierre Trudeau and Mexico's President Jose Lopez Portillo. The performers, unfortunately, were not world-class superstars. Entertainment included Foster Brooks, the perennial drunk on Dean Martin roasts; Sammy Davis, Jr.; and Tony Orlando, with yet another rendition of 'Tie a Yellow Ribbon'.

Film clips showed Ford leading Hope on a tour of the musuem, where among the display of gifts from the bicentennial were an American eagle constructed of beer-can tabs and a copy of the Declaration of Independence done in cheese.

At the end of a very negative review of this show, *The Village Voice* concluded with a note that indicates the intensity of Hope's enduring popularity. This politically liberal, culturally sophisticated paper said:

> In fairness to Bob Hope, a footnote: Hope has recently petitioned President Reagan to throw his weight behind an effort to choke off the insane spread of handguns in this country. That's a show of intelligence and compassion far beyond anything the president himself has yet mustered.[6]

Nineteen-eighty-two was far from Hope's best year. Not only did he suffer a recurrence of his eye problems, but his name was associated with a scandal in England. The following was published in the *Observer* on 12 September 1982:

> In eight days Bob Hope flies into London for the normally pleasurable date of being the pampered favourite celebrity at the Bob Hope British Golf Classic, at which he is scheduled to tackle the pros with a few rounds partnered by his co-celebrity guest, former US President, Gerald Ford.
>
> This year, however, the 79-year-old wise-cracking film star will arrive with the disquieting knowledge that the Charity Commission is conducting an investigation into the financial affairs of the £2 million-plus lavish charity spectacular of which he is patron.

The long, complicated story which followed explained that a benefit tournament Hope supported was costing a great deal while providing very few funds to charity. Hope was not mentioned as part of the financial dealing, but found himself in the unfortunate position of having lent his name to an organization under fire.

Nothing could slow Bob down in 1983, as he got ready to

celebrate his eightieth birthday. Hope Enterprises organized the event and handled the publicity, with celebrations on both sides of the Atlantic. The week before, the Senate got the nod to celebrate Bob's birthday on their floor. NBC devoted an entire night's prime-time programming to the celebration held at the Kennedy Center. In attendance were the President and Nancy Reagan; some of the latest pretty faces to adorn Hope's TV shows, including Lynda Carter, Brooke Shields, Cheryl Tiegs and Christie Brinkley; and such legendary celebrities as George C. Scott, Phyllis Diller, George Burns and Lucille Ball. Sports figures reflecting Hope's inclusion of sports in his shows were represented by Howard Cosell and boxers Roberto Duran and Marvellous Marvin Hagler; and there were other performers too, including Flip Wilson and Barbara Mandrell.

Bad publicity about the financially suspect British golf tournament continued through 1983. Held for the fourth year in a row on 22 September, with Hope and Gerald Ford and various other celebrities in attendance, it was permanently cancelled two months later on 25 November. On 20 December 1983, the tournament's creditors were described as 'surprised' about the state of the finances, according to the London *Times*. The next day, *The Times* reported that Hope denied receiving any appearance fees for the events.

That same day, Hope made a separate appearance in the news. He was en route to Lebanon for his first overseas Christmas tour for the USO since 1972.

On 23 October, the US Marine headquarters in Beirut was suicide-bombed, killing 241 men. The Marines had been stationed there as part of a multi-national 'peace-keeping' force in that troubled country. American ships were being kept offshore, packed with lonely, angry, frustrated men.

Hope took Brooke Shields and Cathy Lee Crosby with him for seven shows on six different ships. As he had done in the past, he made an unannounced visit to one of the most dangerous spots in the area – he visited the Marines stationed on land near the Beirut airport.

His biggest laugh came from his line, 'If this is peace-keeping, aren't you glad we're not at war?'

9

Hope Springs Eternal

No entertainer in history has maintained such a
phenomenal pace for so long.[1]

The older Hope gets, the more attention he attracts. The focus
of this attention these days is not so much on his political views
or talent, but rather how he manages to remain so active. What
makes him tick? At his age, many people are rocking on the
porch, playing shuffleboard in Florida, or in more unfortunate
cases, living out their days in rest homes.

Although Hope has had his medical problems, he has been able
to deal with them. It should be pointed out that he can afford the
very best care, but this is not the complete reason for his longevity.

Hope also *looks* young for his age. His hair is his own and only
a little tint is added for the cameras. Without it, Hope says, the
light would shine through to his scalp.

One explanation for his long active life could be heredity.
Grandfather James lived to be almost 100 years old, and Aunt
Polly was even more aged at the time of her death. Despite this,
however, Hope's mother and some of his brothers succumbed
early to cancer. In view of the conflicting evidence, the answer
would seem to lie elsewhere.

Bob has always been careful of his appearance, and his love of
life causes him to be aware of the state of his physical fitness. He
never wants to give up performing or playing golf, and adheres to
a strict programme of exercise and diet.

Bob begins each day, if possible, with the same routine. Rising
at 10:00 a.m. (after getting to bed around 1:00 a.m. – Broadway
hours), he breakfasts on stewed fruit, juice, decaffeinated coffee
and a vitamin pill. Bob's next step is a little unorthodox: he hangs

from a pair of iron rings for about 30 seconds. After beginning the treatment because of a problem he had a few years ago with a worn-out disc in his back, Hope claims that the stretching has kept all pain away from that source.

Hope frequently skips lunch and usually eats dinner by 8:00 p.m. He tends to eat fast, clearing his plate. His favourite dinner is lamb with mint sauce, mashed potatoes and peas, although he avoids both gravy and bread. As far as desserts are concerned, he admits to a sweet tooth, particularly when it comes to ice-cream and lemon meringue pie.

Bob has strong self-discipline when it comes to personal habits. He was once a heavy smoker, but when his doctor told him to quit, he did. Dolores recalls that he said that a cigarette he was smoking one day would be his last one – and it was, 40 years ago. As for drinking, he does very little. In the past, he says, he loved to drink, but it interfered with his productivity. In addition, the development of a bladder problem caused him more worry about the effect of drink.

For exercise, Bob tries to get in some golf almost every day. Lakeside golf course is just five minutes away from home, and Bob and Dolores usually get in nine holes together on Sundays. He uses a cart, but claims that he does this so he can get in more holes because he walks around plenty at each hole. He also swims, frequently doing five laps in his Olympic-sized pool in Palm Springs. For many, many years, he has had a masseur. Travelling everywhere with Hope, the man gives Bob a rub-down every day at 7:00 p.m. for 45 minutes.

Hope also has the ability to fall asleep anywhere – on planes, in the back of taxi cabs, whenever there's a lull and his attention is not required. This has helped avoid the problems of jet lag on his frequent trips. These days, he's on the road about 100 days out of the year.

His routine on the road is pretty much the same as it is at home. The only difference is that he has a show to perform, but that rarely takes much more than an hour. He continues with preparations for the next television show, and saves energy for the important thing: finding a golf course to play.

On rainy days at home, Hope likes a couple of hours' nap late in the afternoon. His ability to sleep anywhere has been noted by his colleagues. Jill St. John tells an amazing story having to do with Bob's napping ability:

Nothing phases Bob, neither fatigue nor fear. We were in
Vietnam during the worst of it – the winter of 1964–1965, I
believe. We had done a show for the GIs at Bien Hoa and
then we were supposed to fly into Saigon. We got held up
for about 20 minutes because of some mishap involving
Barney McNulty, who has been Bob's cue-card man for five
years.

During the delay, the Vietcong blew up the Brinks Hotel,
across the street from the Caravelle, where we were
supposed to stay in Saigon. Everyone else was spooked out
but it didn't bother Bob in the least. He just went to his
room, which was strewn with shattered glass, and fell
asleep. He has the rare ability to sleep or take catnaps
anywhere.[2]

McNulty recalls that it was later discovered that the blast actually
had been an assassination attempt on Hope's group, and when
Hope learned about it, he said, 'Saved by the idiot cards again!'[3]

Hope also has had the benefit of expert medical care. He
carries the names of doctors in all the major cities he regularly
visits, though he rarely needs them. When illnesses or other
physical problems do occur, he has great recuperative powers.
His worst problem has been the haemorrhaging behind his eyes,
but knowing that this is caused by overwork, he has learned to
pace himself to avoid the problem.

Perhaps the most important ingredient in maintaining Hope's
enviable health is his state of mind, his spirit and *joie de vivre*.
His temperament is evidenced in how he runs his life, his daily
schedule, and above all, his love for entertaining.

His ability to fall asleep whenever his body needs it demon-
strates a remarkable peace of mind. He is relaxed and at ease with
himself most of the time. He doesn't believe in putting things off
and is sure that worrying about what hasn't been done is more
stressful than just doing it in the first place. He also works hard at
staying calm when things go wrong, and doesn't waste energy on
getting upset. But even with the best of intentions, Bob sometimes does allow anxiety to intrude, and people who are used to
working with him have learned to recognize the signals, one of
which is that he begins to sing between his teeth.

His wife, Dolores, who surely knows him better than any other person, agrees that anxiety can sometimes get the better of him, and has noted his special need for recognition. She tells the story of how Bob brooded when he was in China because nobody recognized him. He just wasn't used to walking down the street virtually alone.

Bob Hope thrives on being able to make people laugh. In a brief article for the *Ladies Home Journal* before his eightieth birthday, Bob wrote in response to the question everyone keeps asking him. What keeps him feeling so young?

> The answer: Laughter, the greatest wonder drug of all . . . It needs no prescription, its benefits are felt immediately, it's available to anyone at any time, and, best of all, it's one of the few pleasures left that hasn't been taxed.
>
> . . . I've witnessed time and time again the miracle that laughter can bring. I've seen it in the smiling faces of wounded GIs, I've heard it in the warm sound of giggling children echoing through a hospital ward and I've observed it in the sparkling eyes of oldsters who were able to find pleasure and a renewed sense of hope in the simple act of laughing.
>
> As far back as I can remember, I've always loved to laugh. And though laughter and comedy became my livelihood, they've always been given top billing in my daily life off-stage as well.[4]

The thrill he gets from an audience is augemented by Hope's perfectionism and real love of being active. He believes he'd wither up and get old fast if he settled down, but by staying involved in doing what he loves he remains young. He also wants to keep doing it until he gets it right. Vaudeville taught its players that they were only as good as their last show, and there was a new audience to win over with each new entrance on stage. Hope was and is, in many ways, a Vaudevillian.

NBC is just ten minutes from Hope's home. He works almost every day and usually he works at night after dinner as well as before his late-night constitutional. Occasionally somebody points out that while Hope doesn't really seem old now, he never really seemed young, either. To many, he's always been sort of middle-aged and Middle American.

He hasn't tampered much with the image he's carefully built

up over the years. Newer comedians are moving towards telling long stories or acting out one-person skits. Hope simply tells jokes, pretty much the same way a funny guy at a party would tell them. He's exceptional in his ability to be average. His jokes are rarely hard or mean, although various groups have found some of them offensive. Certainly, Bob has never intentionally offended any audience.

Hope is truly a man of his times. When he was growing up in vaudeville it was *de rigeur* to deal in stereotypes of everyone except white males, and even some of them fell victim as well. Indians were portrayed as stiff, blanket-covered people whose vocabulary consisted of 'How'. Women were either sex objects or housewives or harridans, and blacks were servants. Bob has 'opened up' a great deal in his attitudes over the last decades, although he is still a long way from someone like Phil Donahue. There's little evidence, though, either in his personal life or his performances, that he carries any particular prejudice or malice toward any one group. His attitude towards women could be dismissed, kindly, as 'old-fashioned'.

Gone are the days of the pratfalls and challenge dances. Hope has certainly slowed down his act, although he still brings an amazing energy to his performances along with his innate relaxation. In a review of a 1984 show at London's Dominion, the critic remarked that Hope 'takes relaxation to the extent of performing part of the show while lying flat out on a chaise-longue. He even executes a tap-dance sitting down, letting the drummer . . . do the actual tapping'. The review continues:

> I must admit that I didn't expect to enjoy the evening as much as I did. Films and television had not prepared me for the seamless ease, even elegance, of a great stand-up comic in his natural habitat . . . Not an ounce of wasted effort, not a single misplaced accent, and not a minute too long.[5]

Reporters assigned to write features on Bob Hope these days often find themselves obliged to accompany him on his regular middle-of-the-night walks. He finds himself signing autographs for fans of all ages – all delighted to find one of their favourite celebrities so accessible. He's also an inveterate window-shopper on these nightly strolls, sometimes starting at midnight or later.

Dorothy Lamour has long been used to Hope's excess nightly energy. In fact, that's how she met him. She was singing at One Fifth Avenue in New York while he was starring on Broadway, and he would drop in on her show during his nightly walks.

Years later she lived down the street from him and Dolores in California. Her doorbell would ring at one or two in the morning and there would be Bob, ready to talk through some new jokes. He was even known to bring along reporters to her house in the middle of the night.

Bob doesn't just take these walks when he's home. He does it everywhere. He might be window-shopping, perhaps meditating, but always greeting the fans.

One reason he walks is that he seems to need to come close to people – shake their hands, get kissed on the cheek by pretty young co-eds, have his picture taken with a grinning fan. But whatever the reasons behind his wanderlust, he brings an energy to these walks that often leaves much younger visitors far behind him.

Hope claims that his late-night walking habit goes back to his vaudeville days. He'd pack up after a show, go to the depot and wait to catch an early morning train to the next town. Once at the depot he'd leave his trunk at the station and go for a stroll.

During a walk in New York just before his seventy-eighth birthday in 1981, he explained why he continues the habit:

> I walk after midnight, when there are few people on the street. I'm not afraid because I'm never alone, someone is always near me from my staff. It's a good deal, too, because I can see something I like – like that golf shirt in the window – and tell whoever is with me: 'Buy me that in the morning.'[6]

Hope's clothes are another trademark of the man. Careful of his appearance, he nearly always does his monologue in extremely well-tailored suits which contribute to his image of being fit and trim. But whether it's the influence of the golf course or the lingering effect of vaudeville costumes, he is also given to wearing some of the loudest, most impossible outfits to be found on anyone, except perhaps the young pop singer Cyndi Lauper.

At home, Bob can often be found in a golf shirt and cardigan appearing quite tame, until one looks down to the neon-checked pink and green slacks and white loafers. In his enormous home in Palm Springs, there is a room devoted to his wardrobe that Bob modestly calls a closet. Any denizen of New York's or London's claustrophobic apartments would call it a large living space. This 'closet' includes a whole wall of shoes and racks and racks of blazers, slacks and country-club attire, including a pair of Christmas slacks with mistletoe emblems.

On the more formal side, Hope claims to own 200 suits, and says he favours the Hart Schaffner & Marx and Dior labels. He will admit to owning a couple of electric blue Johnny Carson suits as well. His daughter Linda thinks that describing his dress style as 'flamboyant' is the ultimate euphemism.[7]

Bob and Dolores live in two homes, one in Los Angeles and one in Palm Springs (120 miles east of Hollywood). The house in Los Angeles is a 15-room mansion on six acres of park off Moorpark Street in the Toluca Lake section of North Hollywood. The Hopes' privacy is protected by a 20-foot brick wall, covered in ivy, with electronically operated wooden doors.

Passing through a heavy oak front door into the house, the visitor enters a large hall with a wide, curving staircase leading up to the bedrooms. On the ground floor is the kitchen, a library holding the Hopes' 50-year book collection, a billiards room, and what they call the family room.

This massive room holds a huge stone fireplace, a full-sized bar, a piano and Norman Rockwell's portrait of Hope on the golf course, in addition to comfortable sofas and easy chairs. Bob often breakfasts here in front of the bay window overlooking the patio and grounds (which include a one-hole par-3, 150-yard golf course).

Attached to the house is a two-car garage with two well-appointed guest suites over it. Upstairs in the west wing of 'Hope House' are the main bedrooms. Bob's suite has a dressing room, a study, a bathroom and a bedroom littered with memorabilia, newspapers, and whatever he's working on at the moment. The house staff includes a live-in cook, a daily maid, and a gardener/handyman. When at home in North Hollywood or in Palm Springs, Hope usually drives himself around, although he uses a chauffeur in other cities.

For all his travelling and his wealth, Hope does not have a private plane. When he's travelling for a sponsor, a corporate jet is sent for him, much to his pleasure. Otherwise, because he's such a frequent flier, airlines guarantee Hope his favourite seat (bulkhead) and the attendants generally keep people away from him so he can work or sleep.

Next to the garage is an office block, staffed with Bob's and Dolores' private secretaries, as well as general secretaries. They handle the 200-300 phone calls and the correspondence that comes in each day. Hope's writers also work out of here.

The building also holds Bob's joke vault, containing every joke ever written for him: in excess of seven million. It is priceless, but rarely used. Hope now tends toward current, topical humour in his routines, supplied by a staff of four writers. Hope has an office in this building but rarely uses it, more often working from the phone in his bedroom.

The estate is protected by guard dogs and 24-hour uniformed guards who log each visitor in and out, as well as keeping track of each after-hours phone call. Hope does not have a personal bodyguard. He likes getting close to people too much for that.

The house and estate are worth millions of dollars, but Bob and Dolores will never profit from it. In the mid-1960's they donated the mansion and the grounds to their local parish, St. Charles (RC).

For many years, Bob and Dolores took holidays and breaks in an eight-room bungalow in Palm Springs, a town full of golf courses. (There is one golf course for every 600 of the 21,000 or so residents.) However, since their luxurious mansion was completed there in 1979, they spend a great deal of time in Palm Springs.

Plans were begun for The Hut, as Bob calls it, in 1973. It was to be the biggest and best of all the homes in the area populated by millionaires. Hope approved drawings in May, 1973, for a house that would include a living room with a skylight 60 feet above, covered swimming pools, and a dining room large enough to seat 200 comfortably.

Two months later, everything that had been built so far was destroyed in a fire. A spark from a welder's torch started the blaze. The Hopes received $300,000 in damages through a suit they brought against the construction and insurance companies.

Tragedy then struck again. The designer of the house and his associate were killed in a car crash after leaving the site.

Dolores took personal charge of the project, and she too fell prey to its peculiar jinx. When close to finishing the job, she fell and badly bruised her ribs and broke two fingers.

The Palm Springs house looks like a cross between a scene from *Star Wars* and a stage at the Academy Awards. Built on the side of a hill, the house encompasses 25,000 square feet. The grounds are equipped, predictably, with a golf hole replete with water hazard.

Over the last few years, Dolores has been able to convince Bob to spend more time at home. He now spends about 40 days a year in Palm Springs as well as a great deal of time in Los Angeles. Part of the lure is his passion for golf, which he plays at several of the local clubs, usually Canyon or Eldorado. Both are within 15 minutes of his home in the desert.

10

A Love Affair With Golf

Since he learned the game in his vaudeville days, some 55 years ago, golf has been a major part of Bob Hope's life.

Hope's latest book, published in 1985, is *Confessions of a Hooker*,[1] which recaps bits and pieces of his life as they relate to golf. He admits to a handicap of 20 these days, but no loss of passion for the game.

During his Broadway days in New York, Hope played courses in Westchester, a bedroom suburb just north of the city. After he was married, Dolores frequently joined him. Bob was getting good at the sport and often played 72 holes on a weekend. By 1936, he had already played over 100 courses around the US, and in Bermuda as well.

Hope began making an impression on the Hollywood golf scene within a month of his arrival in the autumn of 1937. Hope and Bing Crosby learned to combine their need for publicity to advance their careers with their love of golf.

On 15 October 1937, United Press announced that Hope and Crosby would 'play for the dubious title of "Golf Champion of the Entertainment World." The loser will work for one day as extra in the other's current picture'. Hope shot an 84, Crosby a 72, which, unfortunately for Bob, was usual in their golf games together.

Hope had already joined the Lakeside golf club in North Hollywood. The course was close to the studios and near Crosby's house. It soon became clear that the Hopes would settle there in the Toluca Lake section. Early on, he also travelled to Palm Springs to play golf.

Lakeside was a favoured course for Hollywood celebrities in those days. One would frequently see Howard Hughes, Jean

Harlow, Ruby Keeler, W. C. Fields and Tarzan (Johnny Weiss-muller) at the clubhouse. The studios also used Lakeside to shoot golf scenes for movies. In fact, Hope's first big movie, *The Big Broadcast of 1938*, had a scene with W. C. Fields on the Lakeside golf course, although Bob never got to play with the older comedian.

Golf has provided a lot of good publicity for Bob and helped him raise funds for charities, but his real love of the game is his strongest motivation. Over the years, he's had some fascinating partners – from fellow Hollywood stars to sports figures, US presidents and golf's greatest professional players. Often the pros gave him lessons. Many of these pairings resulted from playing pro-am (professionals and amateurs combined) tournaments. Having participated in pro-am tours for 40 years, Bob now plays about a dozen tournaments a year.

During his career Hope has played over 2,000 courses, not only in America, but also in Korea, Australia, Casablanca, Japan, Christmas Island in the Pacific, France, Germany, Spain and Thailand. He always brought along his clubs when going overseas to entertain the troops, usually finding a spot to take a few swings. It's estimated that he spends about $50,000 a year in membership fees to golf clubs around the United States and the United Kingdom.

When World War II began, Hope and Crosby put their famous rivalry and legendary golf games to good use. Touring the United States, they raised money for war relief by playing exhibition games.

The two men set off on an exhibition golf tour in February 1942 to benefit the Red Cross and other war relief causes. They played Phoenix, Houston, Dallas, Fort Worth, Corpus Christi and San Antonio. In San Antonio, Hope stripped down to his shorts as a bonus prize for the person who made the largest donation. Winding up in Sacramento, the tour generated quite a lot of publicity when Hope actually won.

During the war, the two played when they could in PGA (Professional Golfers' Association)-sponsored matches, continuing through 1945, when they played for the War Loan Drive.

Hope's game was at its best in the early 1950s when his handicap was down to 4. Crosby entered the British Amateur in 1950 and came back raving about it. Hope decided to try it in 1951 and although he lost the first round, he too enjoyed the experience. The gallery (audience) was over a thousand strong.

When Hope's idol Dwight David (Ike) Eisenhower was elected President in 1952, the golfing jokes began. Eisenhower loved the game, managing to play frequently regardless of the demands of state. While in office, he took 29 trips to Augusta National to play, frequently with Arnold Palmer. He also liked one of Hope's favourite clubs in Palm Springs, the Eldorado.

Bob and Ike began to play together frequently and Bob claims to have been able to beat him regularly. Mamie Eisenhower and Dolores would join in as well, but Hope has revealed that Mamie was a terrible putter.

The two couples developed a friendship that continued after Ike left office. Most of Bob's statements about Ike are humorous, but it is obvious he had a deep personal regard for the man.

Hope has been involved since 1959 with the Palm Springs Classic, a pro-am event set up to benefit the Coachella Valley charities. (Palm Springs is located in an area called Coachella Valley, which includes Palm Desert.) In 1965, he was persuaded to spearhead the annual event. Chrysler and NBC declared that they would participate if the tournament were renamed for the comedian. The event has become one of the highlights of the Palm Springs social season, with all the players and an additional 200 guests invited to a party at the Hopes.

The Bob Hope Desert Classic is held in January, and it has the largest number of participants of any event on the pro tour: 136 pros and 408 amateurs. At four different courses in Palm Springs, the players shoot 90 holes between Wednesday and Saturday. Hope now plays only those two days, spending the balance of the time with the guys from NBC. On Sunday, only the pros play.

Amateurs not belonging to any of the participating clubs pay $3,600 to sign up; members pay $2,000. The Desert Classic is sold out a year in advance, and the tournament turns a tidy profit from these entrance fees as well as the television rights and many extra donations. Seventy per cent of the profits go to the Eisenhower Medical Center, and the balance is divided among 39 charities in the area. The Classic alone has raised $10 million for the Eisenhower Center, and its average annual earnings in recent years have been about $1 million.

In addition to his television duties, Bob is responsible for lining up the 18 to 20 celebrities who will play each year. In 1977, he asked Gerald Ford to appear, expecting the ex-President (who surrendered his office to Jimmy Carter that same month) to show up for one day of the festivities. Ford asked to play the whole event and has played every year since. Hope and Ford have become very good friends.

Bob claims Ford gets the biggest gallery of the tournament, probably fed by jokes Hope has made over the years about Ford's swing. The ex-President is known for hitting his ball into the spectators' area from time to time, and Bob takes full advantage of this in his comedy routines.

The Desert Classic also attracts other major celebrities. The former Speaker of the House, Democrat Tip O'Neill of Massachusetts, is there every year and for many years Dwight Eisenhower always came to present the trophy. The entertainment world is represented by the likes of Glen Campbell, Andy Williams, Charley Pride, Danny Thomas, Phyllis Diller, and Sammy Davis, Jr. The Classic has also seen performances from Pat Boone, Ray Bolger, Telly Savalas, Jack Lemmon, Scatman Cruthers, Robert Goulet, Lawrence Welk, Foster Brooks, Gordon MacRae, Fred MacMurray, Effrem Zimbalist, Clint Eastwood, Flip Wilson and Joey Bishop. In addition, other celebrities have included astronauts Alan Shepard* and Neil Armstrong; Congressmen Dan Rostenkowski, Bob Michel and Marty Russo; ex-Governor of California Ronald Reagan and ex-Vice-President Spiro Agnew. Some of the pros who've played the Desert Classic include Arnold Palmer, Billy Casper, Jack Nicklaus, Gary Player, and Lee Trevino.

Hope's name also has been involved with the British Bob Hope Classic, although it cannot claim the same sort of results for charity. In 1984, Japan instituted the Bob Hope Charity Golf Club, about two and a half hours from Tokyo (or 20 minutes by helicopter from the airport).

Hope receives awards from every conceivable source, and the golfing community is no exception. Among them: The Bob Jones Award from the US Golf Association for Sportsmanship; the Gold Tee Award from the Metropolitan Golf Writers in New York; the Old Tom Morris Award from the Golf Superintendents Association of America; and a silver cup from *Sports Illustrated* on the occasion of his fifth (and last) hole-in-one.

* Shepard claims to have got the idea for his famous golf shot on the moon from Hope when the latter visited NASA and took a swing while in simulated weightlessness.

Around his eightieth birthday, Bob was inducted into the World Golf Hall of Fame. At about the same time, he played in Jack Nicklaus' Memorial tournament in Dublin, Ohio, where the galleries sang 'Happy Birthday' to him at each hole and the organizers presented him with a huge birthday cake.

Hope's most frequent partners these days include Glen Campbell in Los Angeles, and Jerry Ford in Palm Springs. He's had a lot of great golf partners in his life; this is how he recalls some of them:

Jack Nicklaus: 'His career has been embellished with dignity, impeccable conduct and sportsmanship . . .'[2]

Arnold Palmer: A frequent pro-am partner of Hope's at Westchester, Bob calls him 'the biggest crowd pleaser since the invention of the portable sanitary facilities'.[3] Palmer is a five-time winner of the Desert Classic, and has appeared with Hope on TV and in the movies. Bob calls him 'a class act right from the start'.[4]

- *Sam Snead*: One year, when Hope and Snead were paired in a pro-am, Iraq was in the news. Hope asked Snead what he thought of Iraq. Snead replied, 'I never played it. Who's the pro?'[5]

Jackie Gleason: Hope says his old friend likes to gamble, and claims that he putts with a swizzle stick.

Joe Garagiola: A frequent Desert Classic player. Hope says, 'He's the only ex-baseball player able to hit his batting average on the golf course'.[6]

Billy Graham: Hope refers to the evangelist as 'earthquake insurance' at the Desert Classic. 'He always wins, but then look at the help he's got.'[7]

Ruby Keeler and Paulette Goddard: Bob lavishes praise on these two, saying that they were the best golfers amongst the actresses in 1940s Hollywood.

Jack Benny: Hope simply says of his old friend that Benny was one of his favourite golf partners.

These days, Bob watches a lot of golf on television (in addition to professional football and baseball). After watching a match he'll often go over to Lakeside and try out a few of the shots he saw. Bob explains that hot weather doesn't bother him, as long as he can ride in a golf cart. He feels that his game is pretty much the same except that he doesn't have as much power for the long shots.

Dolores is the only other Hope with a real passion for golf. She beat her husband once in Vienna, something he has never forgotten. Dolores claims that Bob still owes her a dollar for winning.

Another member of Hope's family, his son Tony, is taking up the game again after not playing for many years. Hope says it's because his grandson, Zachary, has taken up the sport – apparently with some success.

Bob Hope would probably play golf from a wheelchair if it were the only way he could manage it. His respect is great for a group of blind golfers, whom he has supported and encouraged over the years. Golf is probably one of those elements that keep him so mystifyingly young. He uses it to keep his mind off business.

And golf is still a thrill for him, especially having partners that include heads of state, the top people in the entertainment profession and leading sports figures.

11

A Warm Heart and a Deep Pocket

Volumes could be written simply about the various charities Bob
Hope has aided during his long career. He has long been a source
of help for those whose needs cry out for extra assistance. Some
of the many stories of his largesse deserve special mention.

One of the most touching instances occurred when Bob was
working on *My Favourite Spy* in 1951. A small, somewhat eccentric English vicar by the name of Reverend James Butterworth
was visiting Hollywood at that time to raise funds for a young
people's club he ran in London.

When the vicar came to Paramount studios, he caught Bob
Hope's attention by not recognizing him. The two started talking,
and Bob decided to take him home to meet Dolores. The vicar
told the Hopes about his Youth Centre, which had been
destroyed in the Blitz. If he couldn't raise the needed funds, the
club would close and the teenagers previously helped by it would
have to go their own way.

Hope promised to do a benefit for him. Butterworth went
home thinking that this was just more empty Hollywood talk.

In the meantime, Hope went ahead with his plans to go to
England to entertain. His producer was the famous Sir Lew
Grade. Hope agreed to do two weeks at the Prince of Wales
Theatre on the condition that his fee, reported to be between
£20,000 to £25,000 per week, would go to the vicar's youth club.

Hope wanted to keep the arrangement secret in order to keep
people from thinking he was doing it for the publicity. However,
word leaked out. When Lew Grade had Reverend Butterworth
come to his office to tell him about the arrangements, the vicar
cried.

The engagement at the Prince of Wales was a sell-out, with

enthusiastic crowds that included Princess Margaret, and the show got rave reviews.

One night a young boy, chairman of the club's drama class, was chosen to go on stage to personally thank Hope. His name was Michael, and he grew up to be the very famous actor of stage and screen, Michael Caine. Caine recalls:

> Bob was really great to us kids. You can always send money – but to actually leave the West End and come right down to the Walworth Road, which isn't the Beverly Hills of London, takes a really charming man.[1]

Hope lent 'the Rev' his support for a number of years. When enough money had been raised to complete the rebuilding, Hope was invited back to unveil a plaque commemorating his work. A close-to-tears Reverend Butterworth made a short speech:

> This would have been a junk yard or a ruin, but for you. And you've really come home. To stand here and know that a life's work would have faded – but for you – makes one feel very humble, Mr Hope.[2]

Perhaps it was the hard knocks he took as a poor boy in Bristol and Cleveland, perhaps it was his early brush with delinquency, perhaps it was just his good heart, but whatever the reason, Hope has been a special supporter of young men.

One of Hope's biggest money-raising events is the annual 'Bob Hope Supershow' in Cincinnatti, Ohio. The event raises money for Bob Hope House Inc., a trust for delinquent and under-privileged boys set up in 1962. The centre of the project is a two-storey house with accommodation for 30 boys. By 1981, the Ohio courts had sent a total of 900 boys there to receive a variety of forms of assistance.

The motto of the Bob Hope House paraphrases the Golden Rule: 'If you treat a human being like a human being, he will act like a human being.' There's a sign in the house's driveway which points to 'The Road to Hope'.

For each of the annual 'Supershows', Hope tries to get at least a dozen celebrities. In 1977 he sold nearly 18,000 tickets for a three-hour extravaganza that featured Gordon MacRae, Joey

Heatherton, Jane Russell, Mark Hamill of *Star Wars* fame, baseball star Johnny Bench and Perry Como.

Hope's frequent benefits have sometimes got him into trouble. Among the many appearances he made around his eightieth birthday was a benefit for the Fire Museum. The event, held at Radio City Music Hall, brought in approximately $400,000 but the total available to the cause after expenses was between $75,000 and $100,000. The sponsors thought that figure should have been increased by Hope relinquishing his $50,000 appearance fee to them.

Hope claimed that there had been a misunderstanding. He said that the producers had had difficulty selling tickets and had asked him to appear in order to boost sales. In fact, he had cancelled another date in order to accommodate the firemen. It seems to have been a matter of miscommunication among all the participants involved. Hope continues to do benefits for the firefighters in the United States, and has noted that he does twice as many for free as those he's paid for.[3]

One of the biggest controversies, of course, was the one involving the Bob Hope British Golf Classic, although the problem apparently originated entirely with the promoters. The amounts of money paid each year to charity were small, reportedly funnelled from other projects. In addition, the promoters' cost accounting was quite sketchy.

Hope had misjudged promoters before. Several years ago, a Georgian named Bubba Sutton was raising money for the Eisenhower wing of the American Hospital in Paris. 'Eisenhower' was always a magic word for the Hopes, so they agreed to help out. They joined several of their Palm Springs and Palm Beach friends for a Paris social whirl called *La Semaine Sportive à Paris* (Paris Sports Week), to which each participant contributed $10,000.

Sutton did not manage the funds very well. Expenses began to eat up all the money as a film crew shot the week's events, with Sutton planning to sell the film as a TV documentary.

A few weeks later, Hope saw the documentary in which he had golfed and performed. The film was so bad that he stepped in, got Louis Jourdan to narrate, shot new scenes and supervised the final edit. However, when he tried to find a sponsor, it was too late.

Hope also got into trouble one time with another kind of

public service – the police. In the spring of 1946, Bob worked for four days producing, directing and MC-ing the annual Los Angeles Policemen's Benefit Show at the Shrine Auditorium. The show took place on a Saturday night, with great success. The next day, Sunday, Bob went to the theatre and prepared for the Pepsodent radio show.

In the meantime, Dolores was at home playing hostess to a fair and bazaar on their grounds to raise money for the Carmelite nuns. Many of the events at the fair were games of chance – dice, wheels, raffles.

About an hour after the affair got started, several cars full of Los Angeles police pulled up and actually raided the fair. The cops closed the whole thing down because of 'gambling'. The newspapers were full of the story the next morning. Hope laughed it off, however, and continued to MC the annual Police Benefit for the next 20 years.

When asked why he does so many benefits, Hope often shrugs it off, saying he uses them to practise his latest monologue. It is a rather modest answer, and if this is really the case, then Hope has got in a lot of practice over the years. He is a regular supporter of national organizations like the Cerebral Palsy Foundation, the Damon Runyon Cancer Fund, the Boy Scouts, the Friars Relief Fund and the Red Cross. More recently, Bob became involved in the renovation of the Statue of Liberty. He sat on the 43-member Statue of Liberty–Ellis Island Centennial Commission under Interior Secretary Donald P. Hodel (famous for his highly publicized firing of Lee Iacocca). Hope has also entertained at benefits to raise money for the restoration.

Some lesser-known charities get Bob Hope's help as well. He appears each year at a benefit to help people suffering from Parkinson's Disease. (A wing of the Parkinson's Disease Hospital in Florida is named for him.) At the request of his daughter-in-law Judy (Tony's wife), Bob appeared with Arthur Fiedler and the Boston Pops (with his three-year-old granddaughter, Miranda) to benefit the Wellesley College Building Fund. He gave strong support to the victims of Hurricane Agnes in the early 1970s and is responsible for the Bob Hope High School for Crippled Children in Texas.

In his frequent college appearances, he will often donate his fee to a scholarship fund. He does a variety of religious benefits for all denominations, ranging from the Catholic Church, of which Dolores is a very active member, to the United Jewish Appeal. His clout and personal appeal often bring in a lot of other celebrities as well.

The durable comic can be a real 'old softy'. One night in Fargo, North Dakota, he dropped in to help a local telethon for disabled children. He stayed an hour, talking on camera and answering phones, always urging people to give as much as they could.

Bob's old friend John Wayne, no stranger to charity work himself, said of him, 'I think Bob needles [the average American] into giving a little more here and there than they normally would'.[4]

The telethon in Fargo and another for victims of Hurricane Agnes were not his first. While making the *Road to Bali* in June, 1952, Bob was asked to host American TV's first telethon, at that time called a marathon.

The inspiration came from Vince Flaherty, a drinking pal of Hope and Crosby's. Flaherty worked for the Hearst publishing empire as a syndicated sports writer and managed to get promises of publicity and financial backing from the Hearst organization. The TV 'marathon' was to raise funds for the 333-member United States Olympic team to travel to the Winter Olympics in Helsinki. Olympic Chief Avery Brundage applauded the action.

The schedule called for 14½ hours on the air. Both NBC and CBS carried the event, which was hosted by Hope, Crosby and Dorothy Lamour; it was Crosby's debut TV performance. The broadcast originated from NBC studios in Hollywood with cut-ins from the CBS studios in New York, the location of most of the sports figures who appeared. The guests included Frank Sinatra, George Burns and Gracie Allen, TV's funny-man Milton Berle, the movie comedy team of Dean Martin and Jerry Lewis, Frankie Laine, Donald O'Connor, Eddie Cantor, Georgie Jessel, the Ritz Brothers, Abbott and Costello and Fred MacMurray. There were also droves of sports figures, kiddie favourites and musicians. Pledges from the event came to a reported $750,000 to $1,000,000. In view of the work he has done since for Muscular Dystrophy, perhaps Jerry Lewis got his inspiration here.

Ironically, the 'marathon' ran over in time, causing the *Road* threesome to miss a day's shooting on their picture. Hope and Crosby each had to ante up a third of the cost of that delay.

Bob and Dolores get countless requests for assistance every

year. They set up the Bob and Dolores Hope Foundation to handle these requests and the often unpublicized donations they make. The profits from Hope's successful book, *Have Tux, Will Travel*, all went to this Foundation.

Perhaps the greatest contribution the Hopes make is of their time, and the project that receives the most time is the Eisenhower Medical Center in Rancho Mirage, California. The Center is a short distance from Palm Springs off Highway 111, reached by turning onto Bob Hope Drive. President of the Center for seven years, Dolores now serves as chairwoman.

Bob told his good friend Dwight Eisenhower about the project in 1964 and Ike was moved. Hope donated the land on which the Center stands and where ground was broken in 1969. The hospital portion was finished and dedicated in 1971. Ike was gone by then, but Mamie attended the honours, as did President Nixon, who flew in on Air Force One, Vice-President Agnew, and California Governor Ronald Reagan.

After ground was broken, Bob and Dolores told the board of directors that they would be responsible for raising a third of the $7 million needed for completion of the first building phase by 1971. They booked the Grand Ballroom of the Waldorf-Astoria in New York, paid the dinner tab of $70,000, then filled the 1,500 available seats collecting $1,000 a plate. Hope got Chrysler to sponsor the event and a 90-minute special was produced.

The Hopes also used fund-raising luncheons, telephone calls, and personal visits. It paid off. Frank Sinatra gave $125,000 and also had a street named for him in Coachella Valley, as did Irving Berlin, the Hopes' neighbour in Palm Springs. Composer Fritz Loewe left the hospital in his will all the royalties from his musical, *My Fair Lady*.

After the success of the New York dinner, Hope planned a similar one the next year in Los Angeles with the help of tycoon Walter Annenberg. Through this event $2 million was added to the $2 million already raised.

A large portion of the money raised from the annual Bob Hope Desert Classic also goes to the Eisenhower Center, which now boasts the Probst Professional Building, the Kiewit Building, the Wright Building, the Annenberg Center, the Hal Wallis Research Center, and the Eisenhower Memorial Hospital, with Ike and Mamie wings. There is also the Betty Ford Center, a famous rehabilitation facility for sufferers from drug and alcohol abuse. Many celebrities, as well as others less well-known have been helped there. The newest building in the complex is the Gene Autry Tower. Autry, a former movie cowboy and now owner of the California Angels baseball team, donated $5 million.

Hope is very proud of the Eisenhower Medical Center, which now operates in the black. He thinks it will always be the most lasting legacy of the Desert Classic. It is also a lasting legacy of Bob and Dolores Hope.

12

Loyalties

Throughout his long career, Bob Hope has inspired tremendous loyalty in his colleagues, employees and friends.

The closest and dearest person to Bob, and the most loyal of all for the longest time, is his wife of more than 50 years, Dolores.

Dolores DeFina was born in Harlem and grew up in the Bronx, daughter of an Italian father and an Irish mother. The family also included another daughter.

Dolores' father died early, but there was plenty of family around – cousins, aunts and uncles. The DeFina family was musical, with composers, conductors and music teachers among the relatives. Dolores grew up singing.

A very beautiful girl, she went to work as a model at age 16. Before long she was a Ziegfeld showgirl. Then, at about the age of 20, she began singing with bands under the name of Dolores Reade.

Bob and Dolores met in late 1933, and Bob describes the event as love at first sight. On 19 February 1934, they were married.

In their early years, Dolores appeared on stage with Bob in vaudeville. She'd sing, he'd clown, and the audiences loved it. After the children were adopted, though, Dolores stayed away from the stage while they were growing up. She became the homemaker, and involved herself in Church work and various charities.

Although Bob had done benefits before the two met, many credit Dolores' commitment to humanitarianism as the force behind Bob's ceaseless benefit work.

The Hopes' long marriage makes them a rarity in Tinseltown and in fact, America as a whole, where the average marriage now ends with the seven-year-itch. How has theirs survived so long?

Surely not just out of convenience, for audiences sense the obvious affection between the two when Dolores sings 'I Only Have Eyes for You' to Bob every year on his birthday specials.

Bob Hope is unique. His unflagging energy, constant travel schedule, success and perennial popularity make him stand out even among celebrities. And yet he is no saint. He practically left Dolores to raise four children by herself. He was usually away from home, gone on Christmas, and even when at home, *very* busy. In their middle years together, there was at least one scandal and there were rumours of Bob's involvement in extramarital affairs.

Hope's comedy routines, both on stage and in film, often cast him as a comically lecherous, ogling, middle-aged wolf. Audiences generally understood, though, that as far as the show went, Hope would always be unsuccessful as a womanizer.

The bumbling, unromantic comedy image, however, was challenged by a starlet named Barbara Payton, who claimed in 1954 that she and Hope had had an affair. *Confidential* published an article about it, using interviews with Miss Payton and her friends. Purportedly, the magazine's lawyers checked out the accuracy of the story before it was printed.

Miss Payton said that she and Hope had met at a party in Dallas, where Bob was playing a charity golf tournament, in March 1949. According to the article, 'They hadn't known each other six hours before they knew each other as well as a boy and girl ever can',[1] and after that they met when they could in various cities. Payton said that Hope was 'no Casanova', and that he was 'one of the closest guys with a buck' she ever knew, and was vain, but that he liked her cooking.*

All that Bob said regarding the *Confidential* story was that he was 'no angel'. Dolores has always believed that Bob is attractive to other women, and has some strong testimonials to that fact

---

* All these revelations came at the end of Barbara Payton's short (1949–1955) movie career, which had included such winners as *Bride of the Gorilla*. An ambitious actress, she was better known for her sexy looks than her acting abilities. She had received a lot of publicity in 1951 when she was the cause of a huge fight between Franchot Tone (*Moulin Rouge, Mutiny on the Bounty*) and Tom Neal, tough guy of B-movies, over who had the right to date her. Within a short time afterwards she married and divorced Tone and had an affair with Neal.

from some very sexy women, but she has enough confidence in herself not to worry too much about it.

Dolores is still one of Bob's greatest admirers. Although a private person herself, she doesn't resent living in the spotlight, though she was concerned for the children when they were younger.

Dolores undoubtedly keeps herself busy. For example, in 1982, when she was 72, in addition to serving as Chairman of the Board of the Eisenhower Medical Center, she was a member of the boards of directors of Mutual of Omaha, the Kennedy Center in Washington and the House Ear Institute in Los Angeles. She is also heavily involved in Catholic charities, among other causes. She proudly watches over her four successful children and four grandchildren and continues to make a comfortable home for herself and Bob in their two huge homes in Toluca Lake and Palm Springs.

Visitors and friends are struck by Dolores' serenity. Amid the hubbub of her life, she remains remarkably calm. A very devout Catholic, Dolores evidently finds much strength and comfort in her religion. (Bob is a sporadic church-goer.) She attends Mass every day, sometimes twice a day, even when away from home. She had a small chapel built in the Palm Springs house, complete with altar, pews and kneelers.

Dolores claims that she did not mind giving up her career to raise a family while Bob pursued his. She admits that she sometimes found it tiring and even dull, but adds that many other homemakers would agree that there is nothing unusual in that.

People magazine asked the Hopes' eldest daughter Linda if she thought it had been hard for her mother to give up her career. Linda thought, 'Probably'. She went on to explain how busy her mother is, pointing out Dolores' strong involvement in improving the adoption laws and services in Los Angeles. She also commented on the possible strain on her parents' marriage in light of Bob's constant travelling.

> Sure, it was hard for her when he went off surrounded by beautiful women. But she had made a commitment to a situation. There was always the possibility of divorce. They didn't. It was . . . for better or worse. Now, as they are older, they are very sweet together.[2]

Bob is devoted to Dolores. He recognizes the work she put in, often unassisted by him, in raising their children and thinks she did a marvellous job.

Dolores did take to the road with Bob whenever she could. Generally avoiding the one and two-night trips, she has gone along on those involving a longer stay in one place. When shooting one of their movies in England, for instance, Hope and Crosby and their wives actually shared an enormous country house during the filming.

Now that the family is grown, Dolores travels much more often with Bob. One reason she goes along is to make sure Bob doesn't work too hard. They also managed to take some grand vacations together, bringing along the kids, when they were younger. They still play a lot of golf together, of course, and continue to seem a well-matched and very happy couple.

Away from the golf course, their social life favours private dinner parties. Bob and Dolores have never been regulars on the Hollywood party scene, as testified by Gregory Peck, who has known Hope for years. In an interview, Peck said:

> I know Bob, but I don't know who he is. He doesn't
> socialize much. Maybe in his personal life he's basically the
> same man who appears on TV. In other words, what you see
> is what you get.[3]

Contrary to popular belief, the Hopes do entertain. Dolores' invitations have always been coveted. Guests are treated graciously and the fare is superb.

Because they're so busy, Bob and Dolores don't get as much private time together as they'd like. When they are finally alone, they have a lot to say. What's more, Dolores is a valued critic of Bob's work and her sense of good taste often influences how Bob selects his material.

Hope does his best to keep in touch with all his relatives. When in England, he often arranges a family dinner at a hotel, or stops in for tea with his cousins. (All aunts and uncles have now passed away.)

He also keeps in touch with his brothers' families. To celebrate the Fourth of July in 1973, Bob and Dolores invited the whole American Hope clan and Dolores' family to come to Los Angeles for a few days. They had to rent a school bus to get everyone to Disneyland.

Although Hope got along well with most of his brothers, he had been frequently estranged from his brother Jim. At one point, Jim wrote a book called *Mother Had Hopes*, about growing up in their home. The publishers refused the manuscript without a foreword by his famous brother Bob. Jim abandoned the project.

In another regrettable episode, Jim found himself in a conflict he had tried to avoid. A woman named Marie Mali, who might be called Jim's common-law wife, went to work for Bob as a part-time secretary. Bob hired her as a favour to Jim. In the job, Marie helped catalogue, index, address envelopes and the like. It was 1939, and Bob payed her $50 a month.

When Jim and Marie found out what Bob's income was, Marie decided she was underpaid, despite Bob's assurance that she'd get a bonus. In the meantime, Jim borrowed $1,400 from his brother, which Bob expected to be paid back.

Finally, Marie couldn't wait any longer to get more money out of Bob. Despite Jim's strong objections, she got a lawyer and sued Bob for $50 a week back pay. Bob's lawyers countersued for the repayment of Jim's loan.

The court hearings resulted in a hung jury and the judge dismissed the case. Brother Jack had been in court representing Bob, but Jack and Jim never spoke to one another throughout the hearings.

Even this cloud had a silver lining. During the conflict, a woman named Marjorie Hughes, a recent graduate of Sawyer's Business School, came to work for Bob – and stayed for 31 years. The two always referred to each other as Miss Hughes and Mr Hope. Although Bob is usually more informal, the 'unflappable' Miss Hughes was never anything less than professional in her long service as Hope's private secretary. She always thought she was hired precisely because she wasn't star-struck like so many others in Hollywood.

Miss Hughes took very good care of Mr Hope. When he was the object of a 'This Is Your Life' TV show in London in 1970, his publicity people asked Miss Hughes if Hope should be told in advance. She said, 'You know Mr Hope hates surprises', and he was told about the show. Dolores, who was arranging many of the 'surprises' of the evening, thought Bob was genuinely surprised through the entire event.

Miss Hughes managed a lot of potentially chaotic projects throughout her tenure with Hope. Perhaps her greatest challenge was the Helsinki Olympics telethon, for which she supervised the collection of script material from the mammoth joke vault for the 14½-hour telethon.

Her retirement party, after 31 years, was held in the Hopes' living room. Hope said, 'No man's had a better secretary'. It took a long time to replace her, during which a number of people tried and failed to fill her shoes. Fortunately, she had foreseen this delay and set up an efficient system to carry Bob through it.

A number of very famous people in the entertainment business credit Hope with giving them their big start, or helping them overcome a problem in their careers. Here are a few of those stories.

Sammy Davis, Jr.: 'Bob began using me in his TV shows when I was still doing nightclubs in LA. I used to ask him to give me a big buildup when he introduced me. But a few shows later, he just said, "Ladies and gentlemen, Sammy Davis, Jr." When I came out on the stage, I muttered under my breath, "Thanks a lot." He whispered back, "Sam, you don't *need* the buildup any more!" That was the beginning of my confidence in myself.'[4]

Loni Anderson: The shapely star of *WKRP in Cincinnatti* points to Bob as the first to recognize her comedic abilities, to realize there was more to her than just her looks. It started when she joked with him during rehearsals for the first TV special she did with him. He's used her as a comedienne ever since and she credits him with turning around her career for the better.

Gary Crosby (Bing's son): Gary claims Bob saved his life by hiring him for an overseas tour to entertain the troops when he was going through a bad time in the army. Gary also refutes charges that Hope is cheap, insisting he was always well paid for his work.

Milton Berle: When 'Uncle Miltie' was trying to make a comeback on ABC, a lot of major comedians turned down guest-spots on the show. Hope came on with no questions asked.

Mary Martin: When she came to Hollywood from Broadway, she was frequently depressed and discouraged. Both Bob and Dolores helped. When she got really down they would invite her over for dinner, and they encouraged her to call whenever she got upset. This was all long before she made her first film.

Zsa Zsa Gabor: After an early success in the movies, Miss Gabor's career was ruined by an affair with another man while she was still married to George Sanders. The newspapers and magazines took up the story and soon there were no professional doors open to her. Hope thought it was all ridiculous and offered her parts in his TV specials. She feels that he gave her back her career.

Maurice Chevalier: During World War II, Chevalier had been accused of collaborating with the Nazis. Hope had known him back at Paramount and respected him. In 1945, when Hope was performing in France, he saw Chevalier in the audience and asked to have him introduced. One of the American officers, however, didn't want him brought forward, saying that Chevalier had been a traitor.

Hope looked at the officer and told him that he was not a judge and jury; he only knew what a great entertainer Chevalier was.

Hope brought him on stage; Chevalier sang several of his standards and got a standing ovation. Chevalier never forgot what Hope did for him that day.

Tony Bennett: On the 1970 'This Is Your Life' show, Bennett explained that Hope was responsible for his name as well as his career. He recalled how Bob had hired a young singer named Antonio Benedetti for a tour to benefit Cerebral Palsy victims and has thus launched him to stardom.

Bob Hope is generous not only with his time and his money, but also with his fame. He encourages young performers, and helps those in the industry who need him.

In 1936, Hope was doing out of town tryouts for his Broadway musical, *Red, Hot and Blue* with Ethel Merman and Jimmy Durante. One of the stops was New Haven, Connecticut, the home of Yale University. After the performance one night a young Yale law student came backstage to congratulate the performers, including Hope. That young man was Gerald Ford.

Hope went on to stardom and Hollywood; Ford went on to serve the residents of his home state, Michigan, and the people of the United States over 30 years in Congress. He gained a reputation for honesty and hard work within the House of Representatives, although he remained fairly unknown on a broader scale until events in the early 1970s propelled him into the spotlight.

The Administration of President Nixon suffered a serious blow when Nixon's Vice-President, Spiro Agnew, the former governor of Maryland, was indicted for criminal activity. Mr Agnew pleaded 'no contest' to the charges and resigned his position, the first such action by a Vice-President in American history.

The Agnew resignation occurred in the middle of the Watergate scandal. Nixon's aides had been implicated and the public and Congress were scrutinizing the honesty of elected and appointed officials. Nixon needed a new Vice-President who was utterly free from any hint of wrong-doing, as well as someone who enjoyed the respect of an increasingly wary Congress. In addition, he wanted a person who supported the platform of the Republican Party. He made a good choice when he picked Gerald Ford, Republican Representative from Michigan.

Despite having very little time to become familiar with his new position as Vice-President, Jerry Ford soon found himself facing the uncomfortable task of assuming his boss's job. In the face of escalating criticism and the strong possibility of actual impeachment, Richard Nixon resigned the presidency, and Gerald Ford became the thirty-eighth President of the United States in 1974.

Hope had been close to both Agnew and Nixon. When Ford, as one of his first acts as President, granted an unconditional pardon to Richard Nixon, Hope very much approved.

In February 1975, Hope was one of 24 guests at Nixon's first social appearance after his departure. The party was given by Hope's Palm Springs neighbour and friend, Walter Annenberg, former American Ambassador to Britain. Hope continued to be supportive of the departed president – a loyal friend.

Hope's support of Nixon following his resignation is indicative of the kind of loyalty he has always shown his friends. He treated Agnew the same way. Because of his friendships with so many Presidents, Hope has been called a political opportunist, though his support of Nixon following the latter's disgrace and resignation proves such a claim false.

President Ford and Hope soon became friends as well. How could Bob Hope not be friends with an American president who was an avid golfer? The men had other things in common as well: they were both mid-Westerners, given to plain speech and honest actions; they both loved other sports as well. Hope's son Tony, a lawyer, became a presidential aide during Ford's Administration.

Ford took office at a time in which American citizens' confidence in their government was at its lowest point in history. The US had barely recovered from the divisiveness of the Vietnam War, and now daily television coverage of the Judicial Committee's interrogation of high government officials led many people to believe that the top job in the nation might be involved in the corruption. Everyone in government had become suspect.

Ford, landed in a tough spot, took the situation in hand. He granted Nixon a full pardon, even though he had not been formally accused of anything. Ford drew a great deal of fire for that action because many people wanted to see Nixon brought to trial. Faced with a no-win scenario, Ford took a courageous step and granted the pardon, because in his estimation it was the fastest means of healing the national wound. He felt that the morale of the American people was more important than the affairs of one man. In hindsight, Ford seems to have taken the right action to bring the nation back together.

After the Watergate crisis had subsided, Ford took on the more pleasant task of leading America through the celebration of its 200th birthday. During the Bicentennial, Americans celebrated democracy, their way of life, and freedom, applauded their history and looked forward to the future. Jerry Ford presided over all this, having helped restore confidence in America and its government.

Ford helped create a new sense of well-being in the country by the strength of his personality. Jerry Ford is a *nice* man, and it shows. Unlike Nixon, Ford did not relish imperial trappings. He played golf, he spoke in a down-to-earth manner, he had an utterly charming wife, Betty, and his children were wholesome American kids. Betty Ford confided their problems to the nation, and every parent in America could identify with her. When Betty suffered from breast cancer she courageously spoke out about it to the American people. Her openness probably did more towards bringing that issue into the public consciousness and encouraging check-ups, thus saving lives, than anyone else has ever accomplished.

Ford also got a lot of publicity from comedians. Given to falling down, tripping and stumbling, Ford often did it on national television, something comedian Chevy Chase made a career out of imitating. Ford also experienced trouble hitting golf balls down the fairway on television. Pretty often, they went astray into the gallery, beaning the spectators. Needless to say, Bob

Hope got lot of mileage out of that.

Forty years after their initial meeting at a performance of *Red, Hot and Blue,* Jerry Ford and Bob Hope met again. This time it was in the White House, in the company of the Queen of England. A week after the Queen bestowed upon Bob the honorary title of Commander of the British Empire, Bob joined the Queen and others at a banquet and supper show at the White House given by Gerald Ford.

The guests included Lady Bird Johnson, the former First Lady, Alice Longworth Roosevelt, Telly Savalas, Nelson Rockefeller and Olympic skater Dorothy Hamill. Hope was the Queen's personal choice as entertainer. Bob put the show together and the Queen was apparently delighted with the result.

During the Bicentennial celebration, Hope and Ford saw quite a lot of each other. Hope introduced Ford at the Kennedy Center gala that was the official start of the Bicentennial. Because of a conflicting engagement, Ford put an Air Force jet at Hope's disposal to ensure that he arrived in time.

Ford is a great fan of Bob's, and he honours the work Hope has done to help American servicemen around the world. He feels Hope was a support during his administration, though not in a partisan way.

Following his loss to Jimmy Carter in the 1976 Presidential election, Jerry Ford took up residence in Vail, Colorado, and Palm Springs, California. The former college football player remains an avid athlete, and his two residences allow him both to ski and play golf close to home. Ford and Hope have become very good friends since the President retired.

Hope always has good things to say about Ford. He's one of his favourite golf partners, and although he continues to make a lot of jokes about the former president's golf swing, he actually gives him much of the credit for the growing popularity of the game. The two enthusiasts continue to play frequently for charity during the year, especially at each other's tournaments.

In 1980, there was another Presidential election. Hope was faced with a dilemma, whether to support Ronald Reagan, an old friend from Hollywood and governor of California, or Gerald Ford, who had become a close personal friend. For the most part, Hope stayed out of the public debate.

Ford and Hope remain good friends and continue to serve as exemplary representatives of America.

13

The Road to Big Bucks

Bob Hope is a rich man. In fact, he is a *very* rich man – but don't expect him to admit it. If there's anything the man hates, it's giving a straight answer about his finances or seeing someone else figure them out.

There's no reason why he *should* tell anyone what he's worth in dollars – that is, anyone except the Internal Revenue Service and his wife, Dolores. His reticence on the subject, though, has fuelled the curiosity and speculation that go with any mystery. It's his dislike of talking about his wealth that has made it interesting to so many journalists. Some of their speculation makes Hope angry; the rest he just laughs off.

Like many people whose life began in poverty, Bob Hope has done everything he can to make sure he doesn't wind up poor again. Not only was his family very poor when he was growing up, but he suffered through some very lean times when he started out in vaudeville. Once he tasted success, though, the only direction was up.

By 1929, when the stock market crashed, Bob was making $450 a week. That gave him enough to send money to his mother every week, pay his stage partner, Louise Troxell, *and* have enough left over to buy his folks a new house in Cleveland.

By 1932, the Great Depression was in full force. Americans who still had jobs, whether in office work or manual labour, were lucky to earn as much as $50 a week. Most had to get by on much less. Show business was one of the few industries that thrived as people sought entertainment to help forget their troubles. Hope not only had steady work, he was earning about $1,000 a week by this time.

Bob felt confident enough by 1934 to hire a chauffeur for his

Pierce-Arrow automobile, for he still made enough to put aside $500 a week. He earned the money doing guest spots on radio and *Roberta* on stage. Fifty years later, most people would still be delighted to have enough income to save that much money each week.

When Hope arrived in Hollywood in 1937, Paramount paid him $25,000 per picture. In addition, he continued to earn a tidy sum for his radio work. By now his staff was growing quickly: there was Mack Millar for publicity (who started at $150 a week); Jimmy Saphier, an agent; and brother Jack as road manager/ executive assistant.

As time went by, Hope enhanced his career, creating more work and requiring more staff, but also earning more money. He became producer of his own radio show and hired 'Hope's Army' of writers.

As he became more popular, his prices went up. The publicity was paying off. For his 1939 vaudeville tour, he was guaranteed $12,500 per week plus 50 per cent of the proceeds over $50,000. He broke attendance records and the theatre took in $73,000, which made Hope's earnings $20,000 per week. He began asking $100,000 a picture. (As a means of comparison, the film industry took in $735 million in 1940. In 1986, Eddie Murphy signed a deal with Paramount to make *Beverly Hills Cop II* for $5 million.)

On 7 December 1941, Pearl Harbor day, the *Los Angeles Times* printed an article on Bob Hope's wealth. It was pretty accurate, judging his gross income from radio, movies and personal appearances during 1940 to be around half a million dollars.*

The reason a hard-nosed businessman like Sam Goldwyn would pay Bob Hope $100,000 plus a percentage of the profits for a single film, especially at a time when Hollywood salaries were being cut, was Hope's enormous box office drawing power. He was breaking attendance records with his movies and the studios were raking in the cash.

Hope eventually got a slice of the production pie and then his own company, Hope Enterprises, co-produced his movies with Paramount.

---

* Hope was angered at the time because it was the era of kidnapping celebrities' children. He was afraid that publicity about his wealth would put his children in danger.

On 6 May 1946, *Newsweek* printed an article called 'Hope Springs Financial'. The magazine estimated that Hope would gross in the order of $1.25 million from movies and radio that year. Petty cash came from the $30,000 a year he made from putting his by-line on a regular syndicated newspaper column. His share of Hope Metal Products, which had prospered during the war, brought him about $100,000 in net income annually.

In addition, Hope had dividends and interest from an impressive array of blue-chip investments, annuities, government bonds and a professional insurance portfolio. Like other people who become rich, Hope took care that his investments were solid, conservative and safe ones.

While at times in his life, Hope has made risky investments, he did not do this until he had what one might call 'gambling money' – that is, money not needed for regular expenses or long-term security.

When he felt in the mid-1940s that this time had come, Hope set up several corporations, including one to handle his personal appearances and another for activities not related to films or personal appearances (like writing books).

Despite his great financial worth, much of Hope's wealth is tied up in 'non-liquid' assets, that is, things that do not provide ready cash, like land. For that reason, at times, he's had to go on the road to pick up some quick money in order to pay his taxes.

Hope's tours have indeed been lucrative. One 36-city tour in the late 1940s netted Hope $700,000, or about $11,000 a day. At the end of that tour, both *Time* and *Newsweek* cited Hope as a new millionaire – solely on his movie and radio incomes. However, he still had to hit the road again to get the cash to pay Uncle Sam.

One of Bob's biggest money-makers, though, has been oil wells in Texas. His initial investment of about $150,000 has earned him close to $3.5 million.

In the early 1950s, Hope's first television deal was for his premiere special, with a straight $40,000 to go to him personally, and all production costs assumed by the sponsor followed by four additional shows for a package fee of $150,000. Shortly after that, NBC signed Hope to an exclusive long-term agreement for about $1 million per year, whether or not a sponsor was found.

Hope's pursuit of the American dream of financial and popular success is easy to understand. He started out poor, and early fees were as little as five dollars a night.

With all the money coming in, there was of course money going out. By 1962, Hope was paying out about $500,000 a year to joke writers. However, without these men, there would have been no act.

In the early 1960s, Jimmy Saphier negotiated a multi-million dollar, ten-year agreement between Chrysler and Hope. Included in the deal were three years of 'Bob Hope Presents the Chrysler Theatre', a 60 or 90 minute weekly show of drama, comedy-drama and variety. Hope was paid $500,000 for each show he starred in, and $250,000 for each introduction to a show.

In 1973, Hope signed with Texaco. The attractive deal required seven hours of programming a year, consisting of four or five comedy specials, for three years. For it, he was paid $3,150,000 a year. In addition, he received $250,000 a year to do commercials and act as Texaco's spokesman. Texaco also provided him with publicity, doing away with the need for his own public relations people.

For years, people have tried to estimate Hope's net worth. In 1952, his lawyer said he was worth around $4 million. In 1969, *Fortune* listed him among the top 50 richest people in the United States. He was the only representative of show business on that list. *Fortune* said he was worth between $150 million and $500 million, which Hope declared to be nonsense. He has always said that if *Fortune* could find that money for him, he'd split it with them. He himself said around 1968 that he was worth $25 million.

At one time, Hope was probably the largest landowner in the state of California. He bought a lot of land when it was cheap, often leasing it to the studios for their location shooting. Many years ago, he bought 16,000 acres in the San Fernando Valley at between $10 and $50 per acre, later selling over half of that land for $40,000 per acre. The remaining 7,500 acres were estimated at a per acre value of over $100,000, although the steady escalation of the price of real estate in California probably makes the land worth a great deal more than that now. Hope also owns 1,500 acres in fashionable Malibu and the surrounding area, and another 8,000 acres of undeveloped desert in Palm Springs.

In 1981, Bob Hope paid about $1 million in property taxes.

This makes it easy to understand why two of his biggest charitable donations have been property. Those donations are the estate he and Dolores live on in North Hollywood, donated to the local Catholic Church (which is exempt from property taxes), and the grounds for the Eisenhower Medical Center in Palm Springs.

The estate wasn't the only property Hope owned in the North Hollywood area. In 1938, he bought a plot near Lakeside Country Club which he sold to MCA 25 years later for $1 million.

Hope Enterprises controls a lot of Hope's business investments. He has had a long-standing investment in the Cleveland Indians baseball team, although that appears to be more of a sentimental item that a profitable one. Through Hope Enterprises, he also owned part of Bing Crosby's Del Mar racetrack, as well as a portion of RCA records. (RCA was the corporate parent of NBC, which was recently acquired by General Electric.)

For a while, Hope Enterprises had an investment in the Los Angeles Rams. In fact he once had a chance to buy the whole franchise for $12 million, but he never got around to doing anything about it and the team is now worth $60 million.

When Hope Enterprises was formed, ten shares were worth $1,500. Later, when NBC bought in for 25 per cent, ten shares were worth $40,000.

Bob has the usual assortment of lawyers, business managers and investment counsellors, but he is always the boss on anything having to do with his business. He has the final word on all decisions.

Hope continues to earn astronomical sums of money. In the early 1980s, he was paid $500,000 to do a series of commercials for Cal Fed, a California bank, to be shown only locally. Yet he asks a comparatively small fee of $25,000 for a college or university appearance. The discrepancy may come from the fact that he loves getting up in front of an audience, whereas he doesn't like doing commercials, which he feels take up too much time.

Along with the high income goes high expenses, however. In addition to a million dollar tax tab, Bob pays about a million dollars more in other expenses each year, despite all the perks that go with his line of work.

14

Performance Style

What is style? Uncle Miltie put on women's clothing. Jack Benny pretended to be forever 39 years old, a miser and a violinist. Chevy Chase does the best pratfalls in the business. Eddie Murphy is street-slick and Robin Williams does characters.

Every great comedian has a unique and recognizable style. Who but Bob Hope would you think of when you hear, 'But I wanna tell you . . .'? Who but Bob Hope has his particular swagger as he walks on stage? And who but Bob Hope can give that certain sly look to the audience as he waits for them to get the joke?

Hope's stand-up comedy routine is a series of fast one-liners, almost always built around either a current topic or a put-down of himself.

His material is tame. Hope does not use vulgarity like Richard Pryor or Eddie Murphy. He makes a lot of political jokes, but they too are tame. His jokes about sex deal with his own inadequacies or the physical endowments of lovely young ladies, never the actual act of sex. Although this author couldn't prove it, it's a sure bet that Bob Hope has never said 'fuck' in front of an audience.

What Hope really does is represent the 'middle-American'. He's the guy wearing the funny apron at the backyard barbecue in Cleveland, or the guy at the country club who cracks up his pals with inane witticisms. He's the poor soul who is making it through the rigours of modern life despite his failings.

Martin Mull has a funny routine about 'your average white guy'. What Mull accomplishes with parody, Hope makes real. He *is* 'your average white guy' when he's on stage. Although he stands up and talks about presidents, royalty and celebrities, he never seems particularly impressed with them. The average

American likes to think he would be similarly unimpressed.

Bob Hope is middle-of-the-road on purpose. His TV audience includes a lot of families and he wants to make sure of entertaining everybody without offending anybody.

When it comes to political jokes, Hope makes fun of both Democrats and Republicans. He explains that he does this because he has a sponsor and feels obliged to take the middle ground so he won't associate his sponsor with a particular political view.

Despite all his efforts to the contrary, Hope has managed to offend a lot of people in his career. Their gripes usually focus on supposed sexism and right-wing politics in his comic routines.

Hope's routines about women do tend to deal with them as sex objects (or failed sex objects in the case of Phyllis Diller). He has always had shapely young women on his TV shows, and also as a standard feature of his military tours. His comedy routines generally portray them as brainless, or simply as objects to ogle and leer at. The humour comes from his lack of success with them.

Although Hope's comic persona always strikes out with the girls, he doesn't suffer too much. The implication is, 'Women – who needs them?' This comes across as funny, but it is not a popular point-of-view with feminists.

Bob was attacked most strongly by feminists when he was also under attack for his stand on the Vietnam War. In London in November 1970, he was scheduled to deliver a monologue and crown the winner of the Miss World contest. He was there because he wanted the winner to come to Vietnam with him that Christmas.

In the midst of his monologue, a protest began. Protesters shouted, threw tomatoes, stink, smoke and flour bombs and displayed signs with slogans like, 'You Are Selling Women's Bodies'. Hope was forced to run off stage.

After the police removed the demonstrators, Hope returned and finished the show. He later commented to news reporters:

> You'll notice about the women in the liberation
> movements, none of them are pretty, because pretty women
> don't have those problems. If a woman's clever, she can do
> just as well – if not better – than a man.[1]

Despite the criticisms, Bob Hope has remained an outstandingly popular figure for decades. Most comedians agree that timing is the key to being funny and Hope's timing is flawless.

He has on occasion purposely screwed up the timing on a joke to make it fall flat. That gives him the opportunity to do what he does best. He implies it's the audience's fault for not getting the punch line and it wins him sympathy. He keeps playing off the bad joke. It also keeps the flow of the act going, since no audience wants to laugh constantly all the way through a show. Hope is also a master of the one-liner, and in fact was the first to take it to the level of an art form.

Every so often writers feature Hope in their columns, as do comedians in their monologues, for his reliance on cue cards. It is a question of the comedian's ability to be funny on his own without writers. Is he an actor delivering other people's lines or is he a genuine Funny Man? Most of his audiences don't care, simply feeling that he's funny, and that's all there is to it. But to be fair, it's worth pointing out that Hope is the joke-master. Although he gets help from his writers, he's the one who decides which jokes are funny, and decides how to deliver them and when to use them.

All his writers have insisted that Hope's abilities and reputation were enhanced by them, but Hope was the one with the reputation in the first place. Some have complained that too often Hope has opted for a sure thing, rather than take a chance on a new formula, that he should have tried a wider range of material. When Bob's daughter Linda was his producer, she tried to update his format, but he lost ratings, and she lost her job.

Bob has always worked his writers very hard. They don't seem to have resented it, though, usually pointing out that Hope himself worked just as hard. In addition, most of them feel it was excellent training, and say that the discipline he taught them served them well in subsequent jobs.

Is all of Bob Hope's material written for him? Does he *have* to rely on his cue cards? In fact, he can ad lib quite well, relying on a huge encyclopaedia of jokes he carries around in his memory, like many comedians.

Phyllis Diller discounts the notion that Bob couldn't survive without his cue cards. She has worked with him a great deal and describes him as one of the best ad libbers in the business.

Fellow performers either complain about Hope's lack of preparation for a show or stand in amazement at the limited amount of rehearsing he does. Here's a sampling:

Loni Anderson: Loni is extremely impressed with Bob's memory which she can personally attest goes back at least fifty years in terms of material. She tells a story about how the two of them were driving to a Veterans' hospital when Bob suggested that they do a show for the patients. Anderson was nonplussed, as they hadn't prepared anything, but Bob said there was nothing to worry about. He pulled out a notebook and quickly jotted down a routine he and Ethel Merman had done in the 1930s. They rehearsed during the ten-mile drive, and when they performed the routine the patients were thrilled.

Lucille Ball: While Lucy is a huge admirer of her former co-star, she admits Bob drove her crazy while making films like *The Facts of Life* by his aversion to rehearsal.

Gregory Peck: 'I was in a benefit in the Houston Astrodome with Bob, where he and Cary Grant and I did a song-and-dance act. We filled the stadium. We rehearsed this act – and with Hope you rehearse maybe 15 minutes, if you're lucky. I got a vague idea of the steps we had to do, but believe me, the dance routine was off the wall.'[2]

Sugar Ray Leonard: 'In 1981, Mr. Hope asked me to be in his 78th-birthday special at West Point. . . . Well, I showed up and he was rehearsing with Mickey Rooney. At about 6:00 p.m., I got in the ring and began to work with Bob. He kept saying, "We can do this better. Let's try it over again." Altogether, we must have done it about a dozen rounds. After about two hours, I said to the producer, "I'm getting a little tired. Can I go back to the hotel for a while?" [He] said, "Sure." I said, "How old did you say that guy is?" He said, "He's going to be 78." I said, "How long has he been rehearsing today?" He said, "About 12 hours." I said, "How much longer is he going to rehearse now?" He said, "About another two hours. He's working on his monologue." I said, "Oh, brother! That old man wore me out!"'[3] (Sugar Ray was then welterweight champion of the world.)

As far as using cue-cards is concerned, Hope admits to using them and actually makes fun of it, though critics deplore the effect it has on his performances. The eyes shift away from the cameras and audience and seem to focus lifelessly on some indeterminate spot. It can certainly be distracting for his viewers, and by contrast the pressure of remembering lines can often add a lot to an entertainer's performance. That extra 'something' seems lacking from Hope's performances in recent years.

On the other hand, Hope has always sung, his most famous song being his theme song 'Thanks for the Memory'. Although not particularly well-known for his singing abilities, Bob has made something like 30 records. Some of the songs he introduced were made more famous by others, especially 'Smoke Gets In Your Eyes', 'It's De-lovely', 'Buttons and Bows', and 'Silver Bells'. Few people realize that he was among the first to sing 'Tie a Yellow Ribbon', even before Tony Orlando, because he used to sing it to the boys in Vietnam.

Hope arrived in Hollywood type-cast from his radio and stage work. Most of his pictures had silly, weak plots and Bob essentially played himself, rather than doing any real acting – perhaps one reason he never won any Academy Awards for his work. (He has won five awards from the Academy, but not for any of his movies, nor has he himself won Emmys, although one of his Christmas specials won one.) Hope has played a couple of serious roles, such as Mayor Walker and Eddie Foy, but most of his movies were more like the sketches in his television shows than genuine dramatic performances.

Hope allowed little time in his movies for plot development, treating them like he does his monologues. 'Rapid Robert' goes for one joke after another – the quick kind of laugh, not the kind that depends on a story being told.

Younger generations get their image of Bob Hope largely from television re-runs of his old movies, especially the *Road* pictures with Crosby. Some young people claim that this is the best comedy Hollywood ever produced, and young comic actors should watch it and learn from it; in short, they feel that it's the bible of film comedy.

There's no denying that Bob and Bing had a chemistry between them that made their jokes and gags seem effortless – as if they were just two good ol' boys who ragged each other unmercifully on the golf course, made their families groan at the backyard barbecues, and got their drinks paid for at the club because people loved to listen to the two of them hold forth.

In a world where no man is able to show another true affection, and arm-punching and insults are the height of true, albeit veiled, admiration, a real compliment could be fatal to a friendship. Hope and Crosby played this kind of male world to perfection. They had a real rivalry going between them as to which of them could upstage the other and which could shock the other into silence with the latest ad lib (supplied by private writers on both sides).

However, Hope's movies were essentially elaborations on his comedy routines. One detects the same themes: Hope lusts after girl, girl turns him down. Hope makes fun of himself before anyone else can, audience sympathizes with Hope. But, Hope is never really brought down. Whether in TV sketches, movies or monologues, it is always Bob Hope, the performer, who comes out on top.

15

Bing

Harry Lillis Crosby, like Leslie Townes Hope, was born in May 1903. Unlike Hope, who was born in England, Crosby's family had been in America since the 1600s. Bing's great-grandfather had left Massachusetts for the Pacific Northwest and helped found both Portland, Oregon, and Olympia, Washington. (His mother came to the Northwest directly from Ireland.) Crosby was born and raised Roman Catholic and stayed in that religion all his life.

Like Hope, Crosby grew up in a large family whose members sang together. He got his nickname when he was seven from a playmate who named him after a comic-strip character.

Unlike Hope, Crosby had a good education – he attended a Jesuit high school and then went on to Gonzaga College. He studied pre-law until sometime in his junior year, when he decided he wanted to make music his life (despite the fact that he had never learned to read music). He left school and headed for Los Angeles. From there, he toured the United States and England. Bing took to the taste of bootleg liquor, which got him into trouble on at least one occasion. He was involved in a car accident while drunk that put his date through the windscreen and put him in jail for 30 days. Jail kept him from taking the first movie role he was offered.

Hollywood at this time was just moving into sound. Mack Sennett, one of the kings of silent comedy, decided to spruce up his slapstick shorts by including a 'crooner', a singer attractive to the ladies. He picked Bing, and it soon became obvious that Crosby had a great flair for comedy as well as singing.

Crosby went on the radio in 1931 and was an instant hit. He now commanded $4,000 a week to play the Paramount theatre in

New York. His movie career hit the big time: feature-length films. By 1934, he was on the list of the top ten money-making stars. (He stayed on that list for 20 years, leading it between 1944 and 1948.) He was also doing very well in the recording industry. Because Bing couldn't read music, he'd have a song played for him a couple of times, then stand up and sing it his own way, producing hit after hit.

Bing was remarkably modest. One of his early movie contracts had a clause that provided for him never to have star billing, written at his insistence. He didn't want anybody to think he thought of himself as a big shot. His record producer constantly pleaded with him to record 'Silent Night', but he refused for a long time, claiming that his style would make it sacrilegious. He finally agreed when his brother worked things out so that the profits would go to Christian missions in China.

Bob Hope insisted on having an audience for his radio show, but Bing originally refused one. He was finally tricked into it. Bing never spent much time seeking publicity.

Hope and Crosby met in 1932 at the Friars Club in New York and a couple of months later found themselves on the same bill at the Capitol Theatre. They decided to do a short act together in addition to Bing's singing spot and Hope's comedy. Fortunately, they discovered a particular chemistry between them that allowed them to work well together and delight their audiences.

The classic 'feud' between the two, in which they traded insults on their radio shows and in print, was never planned. The writers started the gimmick, and because it worked, Bob and Bing kept it up. When doing guest spots on each others' shows, they both came armed with a barrage of one-liners from their own writers. Bob made fun of Bing's loud clothes (Crosby was actually colour blind), his losing race horses, and the taxes he paid on his huge income. Bing shot back with jokes about Hope's supposed cheapness, his slight paunch and his lack of success with the ladies.

After seeing their act at the Del Mar club, a movie producer named William LeBaron from Paramount decided that their routine would look good on film. The first *Road* picture, *The Road to Singapore*, was conceived. Dorothy Lamour, the sultry New Orleans beauty, joined Hope and Crosby and a tradition was born.

Each man had his own comedy writers 'spruce up' the script they were given. A total of seven *Road* pictures were made, and they all had roughly the same plot. The 'boys' would get in trouble and be chased by every kind of bad man (especially young Anthony Quinn in the first three of the films), Hope would want the girl, and Bing would get her.

Bob Thomas of the Associated Press wrote of the Hope–Crosby partnership:

> Few partners in show business history complemented each other so thoroughly. Hope was a premier gagster who could sing. Crosby was a supreme singer who was clever with a quip. Hope had started his career as a dancer, and Crosby learned to hoof with a certain heavy-footed flair. But even beyond their superior talents, the relationship was right.
>
> Although they could toss insults with . . . accuracy . . . there was no sting involved. The public believed that Bing and Bob were two men who really liked and enjoyed each other.[1]

And they did. They truly complemented each other, not only as entertainers but as friends. Bob had the energy and ambition, Bing had the smooth confidence. Both were golf fanatics; in fact Bing already had his own charity tournament. He also got Bob interested in horse-racing (Bing started the Del Mar track). They both liked organized professional sports, too: Bing owned the Pirates, and Hope went on to invest in sports teams as well.

Hope admits that Bing was always a little better at golf. They made small bets, and negotiated themselves blue in the face over the playing conditions.

Hope and Crosby were quite different in personality. They did not see much of each other when they weren't working. Bing was given to dark moods, tended to distrust people and often seemed cold and reserved in person, quite contrary to his smooth, affable screen persona. Hope, on the other hand, sought out whatever audience was available. In Hope's early years in Hollywood, when Crosby lived not far from him, they got together for golf at Lakeside. They both had young families and heavy work schedules, and when Bing moved away they saw less of each other.

Hope, who never got over Broadway hours, was amazed at

Crosby, who would get to bed by 9:00 or 10:00 at night, rise at 6:00 a.m. and hit a few golf balls before coming to the studio. Midnight roaming wasn't for Bing.

Like Hope, Bing devoted a lot of time to the war cause in the 1940s. In addition to their joint golf tours around the country to raise money, Bing also toured military bases in Europe on his own. However, Bing was not fond of doing benefits, preferring to do his part for charity more quietly.

Crosby was a loner and had no really close friends. People who considered themselves his good friends were suddenly dropped. Perhaps because Bob Hope never pushed or made Bing feel he was being taken advantage of, Bob was about as close a friend as Bing had. Hope was one of the very few who attended Crosby's funeral, by specific request in Bing's will.

Phil Harris was another of Bing's few real friends. They spent a lot of time hunting and fishing together, activities which never really appealed to Hope.

Bing admitted that he was lazy, and Hope seconded his opinion. Crosby refused to take part in a conversation that bored him, or to spend time on anything that didn't amuse him. He himself said:

> I'm not very effusive. I'm not very demonstrative. I just never have been . . . I don't know why, it's just something I've inherited. I may think a lot of a person, but I seldom tell them so. I'll tell them about their ability . . . I've never told a friend that 'I love you' or 'I like you' and if any friend told me that, I'd be very embarrassed and I wouldn't know what to do. . . . [2]

A number of people feel that Bing's reserve had to do with problems he had at home. His first wife, Dixie, was an entertainer, but after the birth of the first of their four sons, Bing insisted that she remain at home in the traditional housewife role. Yet Bing himself wasn't home much. When not working, he was off at his ranch, hunting or playing golf. Dixie took to the bottle, apparently, for she was said to have a drinking problem. Bing was a strict Roman Catholic, and Dixie wasn't Catholic.

A lot has been written about Bing's performance as a father to his sons from this marriage. He was very strict, and he and Dixie quarrelled about his neglect of the boys. None of them finished university, and all married Las Vegas showgirls.

After Dixie died in November 1952, Bing dated a number of young women, including Rhonda Fleming. He finally settled on a woman younger than his eldest son, Gary. Her name was Kathryn Grant (though she was born Olive Grandstaff). A former beauty queen (crowned at the Houston Fat Stock Show, where Roy Rogers recommended she go to Hollywood), Kathryn converted to Catholicism for Bing. Together they started a new family, and one child was the now famous Mary Frances.

Crosby's new family life was a little different from his and Dixie's. This time, Bing gave Kathryn support when she returned to school and became a registered nurse. His social habits didn't change much, though. After Bing married Kathryn and moved to Hillsborough (outside San Francisco), Bob and Bing didn't see much of each other except for work.

Bing Crosby may have actually been richer than Bob Hope. The two invested in similar businesses and frequently in the same one, like the Texas oil wells that earned them so much money, and the far less successful Lime Cola. Crosby formed Bing Crosby Enterprises to develop the new products. Perhaps his interest in this stemmed from his war years' work to sponsor an effort to develop new inventions, particularly weapons, that would aid the Allies.

Crosby Enterprises perfected a system of tape recording which allowed broadcasts to be taped and played later. It was very successful, and grew out of Bing's desire to do this with his own shows. He also invested heavily in the Vacuum Foods Corporation, maker of Minute Maid frozen juices. American TV audiences may recall his frequent commercials with his family for the product. He produced radio shows and some of his movies in addition to other television series like *Ben Casey*, and *Fireside Theatre*. He owned an 18,000 acre ranch in Nevada that ran 4,500 head of cattle. Bings Things, Inc. marketed a variety of gadgets, and Crosby owned race horses, sports teams and a race track.

Hope considers his work with Crosby a big break for his career. He recalls being cast in his first movie with Bing:

> After *The Cat and the Canary*, Paramount told me to hit the road.

'You can't do this to me!' I protested. '*The Cat and the Canary* was a hit, wasn't it?'

'Now, relax, Bob. We're trying to tell you that you're going to do a picture called *The Road to Singapore* with Bing Crosby and Dorothy Lamour.'

'Yeah, but that doesn't give you the right to drop my option – you what?'

It took a brief period for the news to sink in. What a break to be working with two of the biggest stars in Hollywood![3]

Hope had already worked with Lamour and was a great admirer of 'Dottie'.

Much of the success of the *Road* pictures can be attributed to how much it seemed like the camera was just in the right spot at the right time to catch two wise-crackers having a good time together. There was certainly nothing forced about their performances. They both had their own writers and they'd surprise each other every day. It's those surprises, together with their brilliant come-back lines, that make the comedy priceless.

Bob credits the directors for permitting the spontaneous gags to happen, and allowing Crosby and himself to make a mish-mash out of the original script. Regarding this, Bob quotes Vic Schertzinger, whose director's job came down to doing little more than shouting, 'Cut!' at the right moments. Asked by a crew member if he wanted to reshoot a scene that had been done in just one take, Schertzinger said:

No, that scene was like a piece of music; it was well orchestrated and it flowed beautifully. Maybe the flutes were off-key or the cellos didn't come in at the right minute, but the total performance was great. I could shoot the scene again, but the actors wouldn't have the same spark they had the first time. And if I made a lot of protection shots, the producers would find some way to foul up the scene in the cutting room. Next set-up![4]

Although Bob and Bing, and Bing especially, had had successful pictures before, film historian Robert Bookbinder calls *The Road to Singapore* the most important picture in either of their film careers. He says, 'A modestly produced and occasionally amusing little picture, [it] was . . . the beginning of perhaps the

most successful movie series in the history of motion pictures'.[5]
Singapore was also Paramount's highest grossing film the year it
was released.

Dorothy Lamour recalls, 'It was fun from the very first day. We
were all exuberant about the picture; never dreaming that it
would end in one of the greatest series ever to hit the motion
picture industry'.[6]

When Paramount made *The Road to Singapore*, they had no
plans for a series, although later *Road* pictures followed the same
formula. *Singapore*'s plot was more defined than those of subsequent films in the series, but the three main characters were less
so in the first outing. In *Singapore*, Crosby played a wealthy heir,
keeping his role somewhat conservative. Hope, a lower class
vagabond, instigated schemes and later scrapes. In subsequent
films, Crosby would provoke the troubles, with Hope helplessly
tagging along.

In supporting roles in *Singapore* were Anthony Quinn and
Charles Coburn. Quinn was still going through the years of
struggle that modern actors now call 'learning their craft'. He was
earning $2 a night at private parties imitating Crosby, Louis
Armstrong and Maurice Chevalier.

Historian Bookbinder says *Singapore* is a prime example of
how 'even a third-rate comedy script can be transformed into
something successful when entrusted to performers like Hope
and Crosby'.[7]

The second picture for the *Road* trio, made in 1942, was *The
Road to Zanzibar*, a spoof of jungle films and early Tarzan
movies. Crosby plays a schemer who uses Hope, the dupe, as a
human cannonball. Somehow they get stranded in Africa, run
into endless disasters and are tricked into 'buying' Lamour
from slave traders. Dorothy Lamour's character is named
'Donna Latour'. A highlight is Hope's wrestling match with a
'gorilla'.

In *The Road to Morocco*, Hope and Crosby started making
fun of their own movie-making. They'd step out of character and
become their real selves. For example, as the two are travelling
across the desert on camels they discuss what adventures they
might meet on their journey: '. . . I'll lay you eight to five that we'll
meet Dorothy Lamour. . . . Paramount won't let anything happen
to us – we're signed for five more years'.[8]

Hope starts to explain the plot, but Crosby stops him and says he knows the plot. Hope says, 'Yeah, but the people who came in the middle of the picture don't'.

Crosby wails, 'You mean they missed my song!'[9]

In this film, Bing tries to sell Hope into slavery. It's a spoof of the many Ali Baba and Scheherezade movies of the day. Lamour played Princess Shalmar.

Morocco is filled with sight gags, including one where a camel spits on Hope. It wasn't scripted, it just happened, and luckily it was caught on film. Not so luckily, a camel is an unpleasant, smelly animal and poor Bob did not have a good day that day.

Morocco also called for lots of ornate costumes. Edith Head, Paramount's brilliant designer, recalled that Bing always complained about having to wear costumes while Bob loved them. Head always thought Hope was a natural costume man with 'the average perfect male figure'. She thought he could be very elegant.

Next on the *Road* map was *The Road to Utopia*, taking place in the arctic and the only one of the series to place our heroes in another time. It's set at the turn of the century and the boys are running around in the Klondike. Despite its period setting, the gags are contemporary. When they lose an Amateur Contest, Hope quips, 'Next time I'll bring Sinatra.' Travelling by dogsled, they see a mountain in the distance. Hope comments, 'Bread and butter.'

'That's a mountain,' Crosby contradicts him.

Hope has the last word. 'Looks like bread and butter to me.' As he speaks, a halo of stars forms around the mountain, making it like the Paramount trademark.[10]

Utopia offered its viewers non-stop lunacy. It also lets Hope actually make off with Lamour for once, happy until Crosby returns years later. The audience sees that Bob and Dorothy's son is the spitting image of Bing. Hope looks at the camera and dead-pans, 'We adopted him.'[11]

Utopia also features one of Hollywood's classic comedy lines. Bob and Bing are posing as ruthless killers in a Klondike bar and Bing keeps reminding Bob to 'act tough'. The rough bartenders asks the boys what they'll have.

'Couple of fingers of rotgut,' growls Crosby.

Hope opens his mouth and out comes a falsetto voice. 'I'll take a lemonade . . .' Bing kicks him. '. . . in a dirty glass!'

In 1948, the three rejoined for *The Road to Rio*, a more

traditional musical comedy. In *Rio* they played carnival rats. The 'bad guys' chasing them this time are the fathers and brothers of young ladies they supposedly compromised. They stow away on a ship to South America, where they meet heiress Lamour. Rescuing her from a forced marriage, they ask which of them she'll marry. She picks Hope, surprisingly, until Crosby learns that Hope had hypnotized her first.

Crosby, Hope and Paramount each owned a third of this picture, and each put up a million dollars for the production. When it hit the theatres, they more than doubled their money.

After a rest of five years, there was *The Road to Bali*. The first of the series to be shot in colour, this was the sixth and last to be made for Paramount. Anthony Quinn was brought back to play the heavy, with appearances by Crosby's brother Bob, Jane Russell, young Caroline Jones, and, fresh from his Academy Award for *The African Queen*, Humphrey Bogart.

Again, the comedy is madcap, zany and fantastic. The boys play vaudevillians diving for buried treasure. This time, Crosby not only gets Lamour, but Jane Russell as well. Bob is so distraught that he tries to stop the closing graphics from appearing on the screen.

Bali is usually judged to be one of the weaker *Road* pictures. The 'ad libs' tend to sound contrived and forced. One of the better lines in the picture has Dorothy Lamour asking if the two always fight over women. Bing says, 'Why not? We never had any money.'

By now, all the world knew that both men were millionaires, so Hope turned to the camera and said, 'That's for Washington.'

The last of the series was *The Road to Hong Kong*. Lamour is just a guest star in this picture, with Joan Collins playing the girl who gets chased. Other guests include Peter Sellers, David Niven, Frank Sinatra, and Dean Martin. Crosby and Hope, playing dancers, get involved in an international plot to steal a formula for rocket fuel. *Hong Kong*, shot in England, was a disappointment to the critics, but was the top-grossing film of 1962.

Another *Road* picture was planned, *The Road to the Fountain of Youth*. Lamour would have been reunited with the feuding duo. However, Crosby passed away before it could be made.

The early success of the *Road* pictures established Hope and Crosby as the most popular comedy team on the silver screen.

They were responsible for huge box office returns. Their success together brought them success apart. They became hot properties, together or apart.

Not only was their 'chemistry' right; their timing was, too. Escapist entertainment was just the right thing during World War II.

Paramount put every star it could find into a musical spectacular called *Star Spangled Rhythm* during the War, and Crosby had a small scene in which he brings his eldest son, Gary, onto the lot. The guard asks young Gary if he has come along to watch his dad work. Gary replies, 'Nah. Dorothy Lamour's workin' today.' Crosby puts his arm around his son and says that the boy 'listens to Hope too much.'[12]

Hope and Crosby were very different about their families. Bob and Dolores' children were kept out of the spotlight as much as possible, but Crosby's four boys were dressed in matching outfits and paraded before the press. Crosby also brought his families on stage with him.

Besides the *Road* pictures, Crosby frequently made 'cameos', or walk-ons, in Hope's films. The two also made cameos together in other people's films. Crosby showed up in Hope's *My Favourite Blonde* in 1942. Hope is fleeing from thugs, but stops to ask directions from a lounging Crosby. A year later in the all-star *Star Spangled Rhythm*, Hope tells Betty Hutton about it:

> Did you see that nice shot I gave Crosby in *My Favourite Blonde*? You know, I like to throw all the work his way I can, because those kids eat like horses.[13] [Jokes about Crosby's kids were a favourite of Hope's.]

In *The Princess and the Pirate*, Hope spends the whole movie pursuing Virginia Mayo. At the end, just when it seems as if he'll succeed in winning her heart, Crosby saunters onto the scene out of nowhere and takes Mayo into his arms. Hope stares at the camera, visibly annoyed, and says:

> This is a fine thing! I knock my brains out for nine reels and then some bit player from Paramount comes on to grab all the goods. This is the last picture I do for Goldwyn![14]

In 1947, both Bob and Bing showed up in another 'all-star'

musical called *Variety Girl*. They appear as themselves and do a golfing gag.

When Hope did *My Favourite Brunette* in 1947, one of his most entertaining movies, he again is visited on the set. A simple man who gets involved with a bunch of bad guys who set him up for a murder rap, Hope is led away to the gas chamber. Dorothy Lamour produces information that saves his neck. The executioner storms off in anger when he hears Bob will live. Only then do we learn that the executioner turns out to be Bing Crosby. Bob turns to the camera and says, 'Boy, he'll take any kind of a part.'

If you look carefully at Cecil B. DeMille's *The Greatest Show on Earth*, you'll see Hope and Crosby sitting in a movie audience otherwise made up entirely of children.

Crosby also showed up in Hope's *Son of Paleface*, which again starred Jane Russell.

Hope and Crosby returned a favour to the comic duo of Dean Martin and Jerry Lewis and did a cameo in their *Scared Stiff*.

When Hope made *Alias Jesse James*, a Western farce, in 1959, Crosby made a surprise appearance, as did Gary Cooper, Gene Autry, Roy Rogers, and from television, James Arnes (Matt Dillion), Hugh O'Brien (Wyatt Earp), Ward Bond (Major Adams), Gail Davis (Annie Oakley), Jay Silverheels (Tonto), and James Garner (Maverick).

Because so many of Crosby's own films were more serious, Hope didn't get much of an opportunity to pay Crosby back with cameos.

Although the two didn't see each other very frequently in Bing's latter years, his death was a great blow to Hope. Years later, Bob still felt that 'a part of my life went with Bing. I still miss him and always will, just like the rest of the world. I remember the good times with him, and they'll be with me always.'[15]

16

Hope for the Fighting Man

Bob Hope's history of entertaining the American fighting man began in World War II and has continued through the recent 'peace keeping' in Lebanon. He is not the only entertainer to give his time and energy to this effort, but he is surely the most well-known.

He has been both praised and criticized for his activities. On one hand, his boundless energy, his ability to bring other stars with him, his clear refusal to stop in the face of danger, and his unrelenting dedication have brought him honours, gratitude and admiration.

On the other hand, his use of the trips for publicity purposes, and his involvement in the politics that contributed to the need to send troops abroad, have brought him the worst criticisms of his career.

Why has he devoted so much of his time to entertaining the military? Was it just good publicity? Did he get a kick out of the fame and honours it earned him? Or was he in fact morally and sympathetically motivated?

There is probably no better answer to these questions than the one he himself gave in the preface to his book, *I Never Left Home*. He wrote:

> I saw your sons and your husbands, your brothers and your sweethearts.
> I saw how they worked, played, fought, and lived. I saw some of them die. I saw more courage, more good humour in the face of discomfort, more love in an era of hate, and more devotion to duty than could exist under tyranny. . . .
> I didn't see very much. And God knows I didn't do any

fighting. But I had a worm's eye view of what war is. . . .

All I want you to know is that I did see your sons and your daughters in the uniforms of the United States of America . . . fighting for the United States of America.

I could ask for no more.

That, of course, was written about World War II. Hope was deeply moved by what he saw on his tours. From his very first trip, he developed a loyalty and a commitment to the Armed Forces that has never dimmed. The troops he entertained smothered him with gratitude. Many sad and tired faces lit up after Hope made them laugh at the situations they found themselves in. He couldn't let them down: he had to keep doing it.

Hope gives a lot of credit to all the other performers who did the same thing, and admits that he used publicity, although he points out that he was not the only one who benefited from the publicity. As Hope brought the experience of war back to the people at home, the service people he visited benefited as much as the comedian from the publicity.

Speaking for all the entertainers who went abroad in time of war, Hope said:

All of us could have stayed at home, worked paying audiences, and had things a lot easier. But you had to face those [military] audiences and hear the reactions of laughs and cheers to realize how we were paid off.[1]

Hope's first military show was in 1941 when he brought his radio show to March Field army base. The reaction of the soldiers convinced him to keep working that audience. They cheered and clapped and showed more enthusiasm than almost any audience before. Between May 1941, and June 1948, only two of Hope's radio shows were performed before civilian audiences. The show's listeners also liked what Hope was doing and sent his show to the top of the charts, where it stayed.

His first long-distance trip was to bases in Alaska. Dolores came along, and within 48 hours, they had cheered up lonely, homesick airmen with seven two-hour shows. As he left, Bob's cry was, 'Be happy, you guys. Be proud! You know what you are – you're God's frozen people.'[2] Those cold, tired airmen went back to their posts with lighter hearts. And although Bob and Dolores had missed Christmas with their own kids, they'd warmed the hearts of a lot of other mothers' sons.

In the midst of the war, Hope took off on his three-month tour of Europe and North Africa. The trip was dangerous and gruelling and exhausting.

Many of the stops on the tour were hospitals. Hope would walk by the beds and talk to the wounded individually. One of his favourite lines was, 'Did you see our show – or were you sick before?' or 'All right, fellas, don't get up.'

Once back home, Hope was a sobered man. A golfing buddy remembers how Bob would talk in the locker-room about the tour. Hope called it 'the most wonderful experience of my life' and said, 'I wouldn't trade it for my entire career. Until you've actually seen them in action, you have no conception of their courage. And that noise – that terrifying noise of battle – is awful. I don't know how those kids stand it day after day, but they do.'[3] Bob's obvious sincerity moved a number of listeners to tears.

Hope called his book about his World War II experiences *I Never Left Home* because everywhere he went, he ran into fellow performers he knew. It was his way of acknowledging he didn't deserve all the credit for entertaining the troops.

The first 100,000 copies of the book were printed as an eight-ounce paperback so it could be sent to military personnel overseas.

On D-Day, Hope was making the last 'Pepsodent' radio broadcast of the season. He abandoned his usual opening to give a speech, honouring all the young men who had fought for all of us.

Hope didn't neglect the men and women in uniform after the war ended. He went to Berlin in the middle of the airlift, flying in dangerous blizzard conditions, to entertain severely demoralized troops. During the show, a sergeant from Armed Forces Radio came up to beg Hope to talk on the radio to everyone who couldn't see him in person. Hope finally got away from his colleagues at midnight and went over to the radio station. The sergeant nearly fell out of his chair when he saw that Bob Hope was actually going to do as he'd suggested. When Hope took over the mike, the sergeant disappeared. When he finally returned, Hope asked him where he'd been.

The sergeant replied that he'd gone to wake up all the other disc jockeys. He wanted to make sure they heard the broadcast because he didn't believe anyone would take his word for what happened.

In 1950, North Korean troops crossed the 38th Parallel and surrounded Seoul. Hope wanted to go to Japan to promote his latest movie, *The Paleface*, and decided he could entertain the troops in Korea and visit Japan on the same trip.

In Seoul, thousands of GIs sat, some in freezing mud, for an hour in the biting cold and fierce wind to wait for Hope and his show. After his last show in Korea, a young soldier asked him for his Army-issue parka. Hope immediately took it off and gave it to the boy, and soon the entire troupe had given their parkas to the freezing boys.

Hope's patriotism was strong and clearly defined. In World War II, since the lines between right and wrong were so sharply drawn, nearly all Americans shared his views. Beginning with Korea, and again later with Vietnam, Hope remained certain that America was right, dead right, and the other side was both wrong and dangerous, but this view was no longer shared by the entire nation.

Hope's strong political convictions were matched by his love of the men and women who risked their lives to fight in these wars. He thought every one of them was a hero. The cause *had* to be right: these young people *couldn't* be risking their lives for an unjust, ill-conceived, or, worst of all, unwinnable war.

In Christmas of 1954, Hope went to the Arctic Circle and Greenland. It was the first of the troupe shows filmed by television cameras and then edited into a special. Hope's guests were Hedda Hopper, William Holden (fresh from his Oscar for *Stalag 17*), and the then unknown Anita Ekberg. Every Christmas tour from then on was turned into a TV special.

Hope received a fair amount of criticism for these specials. He was accused of 'exploiting conflict' and 'cashing in on human misery'. Criticism of this sort was strongest during the Vietnam War. It's quite true that the shows helped toot his own horn, but they also were sponsored. Sponsors' money helped pay for the trips. The USO put up some funds for each trip, American taxpayers supplied the transportation, but a lot of the costs were borne by Hope himself, and the sponsors helped him.

Considering all the danger Hope ran into on his military tours – bombs, grenades, shotguns and more – it's ironic that his worst injury was caused during peacetime in Labrador by a woman he had brought along as part of the troupe. Her name was Joan Rhodes.

Rhodes was a strong-woman. Hope saw her act in England and brought her along. She was very attractive and very strong indeed. The routine called for Hope to sing 'Embraceable You' while Rhodes walked seductively out on stage, picked up Hope as though she were King Kong with Fay Wray, and cuddled him while he sang. It worked well in rehearsals, and Hope decided it would be even better if Rhodes lifted him over her head.

When the show actually went on Rhodes tried to do just that. Hope stood on her hands, but then she began to falter, and Bob was thrown onto the cement floor. The audience laughed, thinking it was part of the act, but a bruised Bob knew it was for real.

A year later, Hope returned to Alaska, this time with Ginger Rogers. In one sketch, Ginger was supposed to hit Bob over the head with a bottle. It was a prop-bottle, supposed to shatter on impact. Unfortunately, the bottle froze in the cold weather. When Ginger bopped him, the bottle didn't break, but it did stun Bob momentarily. Ginger thought he was acting, so she hit him again. He slumped to the floor, although everyone, including Ginger, thought he was still acting. When he came to, he kept the sketch going and didn't make anything of having been knocked out.

For Christmas of 1957, Hope toured the Pacific with Jayne Mansfield, who posed for pictures in a pink-furred bikini. Cardinal Spellman, who was also known for his overseas Christmas tours, visited some of the same spots, although at different times.

On that tour the troupe played two bases along Korea's 38th Parallel under extreme conditions. At one, men watched the show huddled in the snow on the side of a hill. The musicians took turns going offstage to warm up their hands so they could play.

At the second stop, the fog was coming in, it was snowing, and the temperature was $-5°F$. The helicopter pilots warned Hope to keep his show short, but he found he couldn't tear himself away from his delighted audience, adding one routine after another until he eventually had to be dragged off-stage and into the waiting chopper.

In the early 1960s, Hope became increasingly concerned about the global political situation. The United States had a showdown with the Soviets over Cuba; the Berlin Wall went up; the Congo was in revolt – in fact much of the face of Africa was changing. Of critical importance to the United States, the problems in Laos and Vietnam were beginning to escalate, and as Hope began to air his views on these events, his career entered a period of deep controversy.

For Christmas of 1964, Hope and his troupe went to Vietnam, marking Bob's twenty-first year of entertaining GIs. When he was cleared to go, he told reporters he was eager. He believed that America would 'push back the Commies'.

Hope had never been in so dangerous a place. The troupe arrived at the first stop on an airstrip pockmarked by shells with the debris of ruined planes alongside it. Security was enormously tight. As many men guarded the perimeter of the base as sat to watch the show.

On the road to the next stop, the performers rode in cars driven by fully armed MPs, while Jeeps carrying machine-gun toting soldiers ran interference against possible attack. After the troupe reached their hotel, and discovered that it had been bombed, the army asked if Bob would prefer cancelling his stop in Saigon and moving on to someplace safer.

Hope decided to stay. At a reception, the NBC newsman Garrick Utley asked Hope if he planned to visit the men wounded in the attack on his hotel. Hope did, and went into the burn ward where medical personnel were removing shards of glass from badly burned bodies. He found the experience at once horrifying and uplifting, as he saw the courage and good humour with which the men endured their suffering.

Hope's TV special about that 23,000 mile tour was really something special. Focusing on the GIs, it showed them sitting in mud, hanging from trees and poles, and standing on trucks and rooftops to watch the show. Its most poignant scene featured close-ups of face after face, crying, smiling, singing 'Silent Night'.

By now, Hope's Christmas tours took six months to pull together. The USO coordinated with the Joint Chiefs of Staff, the itineraries were worked out and revised, equipment was found and advance men were sent. Stars were cast, security was arranged, a battery of vaccines were injected into veins, and writers worked overtime. The whole operation would cost Hope about $50,000.

He felt paid back by the response he got from the service men and women. Far from home and all they loved, away from anything familiar, living with constant fear of injury and death, forced to view atrocities no society should ever permit, these young people embraced Bob Hope with open hearts.

Each member of the audience was lonely. Bob became their friend. Each was depressed. Bob cheered them up. Each was homesick. Bob brought them the familiar and the ordinary. Each felt forgotten in some way. Bob had come to them.

The tours were not easy for the cast and crew. The work was hard and long. Surprisingly, however, many made the trip year after year. There was a special spirit to the trips that kept bringing them back.

Because of his experience with the soldiers, sailors and marines in the war zone, Hope was baffled when he got home to the US. He seems to have felt that the protest against the war was a protest against the courage and self-sacrifice of the people fighting it. He thought Americans were betraying these boys. Any argument that said either that the government shouldn't have sent them there in the first place, or that they themselves should have refused to go, just wasn't acceptable to him.

In his book, *Five Women I Love: Bob Hope's Vietnam Story*, he made clear his views of that war and his scorn for those who opposed it:

> I might as well admit it. I have no politics where the boys are concerned. I only know they're over there doing a job that has to be done, and whatever is best for them is best for me. I bow to no man in my love for my country, and if my zeal for backing these kids to the hilt means offending a few part-time citizens and thereby losing a few points in the Nielsen, so be it. . . .
>
> And the thing that never stops amazing me is the good grace with which they accept their impossible roles. A soldier stands in the twilight between his civilization and the raw savagery of war. . . . These kids seem to be a lot more optimistic about this commitment than a lot of our citizens here at home. In their everyday job of fighting this treacherous war they know there's no alternative. . . .
> They're not about to give up – because they know [that] if they walked out of this bamboo obstacle course, it would be like saying to the Commies – 'Come and get it.'

Of course, that sentiment is what caused so much protest against Hope. Dissent is a privilege of democracy. Disagreement with the policy of a particular Administration is neither disavowal of the American Constitution nor support of Communism. It is in fact the opposite. Loyalty to the government and society that makes up America does not necessarily require supporting a war against one's own conscience.

Bob Hope may have equated dissent with disloyalty, but he was truly sincere in his respect for the American military. He believed in them so strongly, thought them so honourable, heard such approval in their applause that he honestly could not conceive of legitimate disagreement. When morals collide, there is no right answer.

From 1966, Hope's family joined him on the Christmas tours. That year Dolores sang 'White Christmas'. Even the two youngest Hopes, Nora and Kelly, came along. All Hope wanted was an end to the war as soon as possible, done in a way he and his friends (generals and presidents) considered honourable.

By 1967, anti-war feelings had escalated to a point that caused Hope difficulty in finding stars to go to Vietnam with him. People suddenly found that they had more pressing engagements. The USO, too, was having trouble getting performers to go to Vietnam. Raquel Welch, however, was not one of these.

Miss Welch's first show with Bob was at the Da Nang air base. There were big signs nominating Bob and herself for president and when Bob came on stage and did his famous golf swing there was a tremendous roar from the massive crowd. Welch was overwhelmed.

The Vietnam War and the protests against it continued. Johnson chose not to run for re-election and Nixon was elected President. Hope embroiled himself in controversy, especially concerning the one-day nationwide boycott of university classes by professors and students in October, 1967. And he kept going back to Vietnam.

When Hope went to do a show at the University of Washington in Seattle, he was picketed, peacefully, by 700 anti-war protestors. One of the demonstrators, a faculty member, told a *Seattle Times* reporter, 'Bob Hope represents one of the better known hawks in this country and I think we're all here in response to that. But this vigil stresses peace domestically as well as on foreign fronts. So it is not so much anti-Hope as it is pro-peace.'[4]

Hope told a reporter that night, 'Hell, I'm for peace – but not at all costs. Why don't they march against the North Vietnamese? Why don't the dissidents march against them? Lots of our kids are being killed. And who's doing the killing? The Communists are the ones who need the demonstrations.'[5]

With the arrival of the seventies, Hope's reception in Vietnam grew less enthusiastic. At Camp Eagle in 1970, he performed for an audience of 18,000. His latest topical humour concerned marijuana and these jokes got loud laughs and cheers.

But the laughter stopped when he introduced the Vice-President of South Vietnam as 'a very great man'.

The following year was still worse in Vietnam. Morale was very low. The War had become a miserable affair. About 50 per cent of all gunshot wounds were caused by GIs, not North Vietnamese. In three years, there were 500 reported cases of officers being 'fragged' – attacked with fragmentation grenades by their own men.

Outside the stadium where Hope was holding his show that year, soldiers picketed with signs like: 'The Vietnam War Is a Bob Hope Joke.' Inside, the cameras recorded the boos for the officers and their wives and the placards being held up by soldiers in the audience: 'Peace Not Hope', 'Merry Christmas Nixon, Wish You Were Here', and 'We're Fonda, Hope'. His jokes about homosexuals and Women's Liberation brought no laughter, only an embarrassed silence. When a general rose to give Bob recognition, many dozens of black soldiers got up conspicuously and walked out.

It was also in 1971 that Bob made his personal bid to obtain the POWs' release. Senator George McGovern had this reaction:

> While Bob Hope acts as an emissary of the President in seeking the release of our prisoners, the Air Force acts as the true Nixon instrument in guaranteeing that the number of American POWs will be increased.[6]

The Christmas of 1972 was Hope's last in Vietnam. Partly because of his efforts for the POWs, his reception was much more pleasant. The war was winding down. In fact, it soon ended, with the American withdrawal being followed by a North Vietnamese takeover which the 'hawks' had considered unthinkable, but many 'doves' had thought inevitable from the beginning.

Passions have subsided since the war, and Hope has recovered friends he lost in that era. Just as many people have now decided that the Vietnam veterans are heroes, and many now credit Hope for his patriotism.

In fact, Hope *did* argue about the rightness and wrongness of the war. In *The Last Christmas Show* he wrote, 'Let no one tell you that when JFK and LBJ sent Americans to Vietnam it wasn't to keep all of Indochina from toppling over like a row of dominoes. Let no one kid you that Communist China and Russia weren't our real reason for being there'.[7]

In 1973 and 1974, Hope toured veterans' hospitals, thus ending 33 years of continuous USO service. He had earned a vast number of awards and had brought a touch of home to servicemen and women around the world, often in the face of great danger.

Bob came out of his 'military retirement' in 1983, at the age of 80. The 'soldier in greasepaint' went back on the road to visit the troops in Lebanon. The Associated Press reported that Hope, dressed in Marine fatigues, told the men at the Beirut airport that he had been warned against going to a place with dangerous, armed men.

'Yes, I'm glad I'm not going to Los Angeles,' added Hope, and the Marines let out a huge roar of laughter.

In an interesting footnote, Bob had desired to do an overseas tour before the Beirut visit. The *New York Times* reported on 1 July 1980 that Hope had wanted to do a show for the Americans held hostage in Iran after the fall of the Shah and the rise of the Ayatollah. Negotiations to make that visit had begun, but were broken off when the United States expelled Iranian citizens in America.

The proposed Iranian visit confirms yet again that whatever the dangers and whatever the criticisms, Bob Hope will go wherever he feels he's needed.

17

Congratulations, Bob!

Bob Hope passed the 80-year-old mark in 1983, but this did little to slow him down. As 1984 rolled around, he was just returning from Beirut. His first job was to edit the footage from that trip into a TV special.

The show aired in January to very enthusiastic reviews that remarked not only on the actual entertainment, but on the thrill of seeing Bob Hope doing one of the things he has always done best. Here's what *Variety* wrote:

> The sight of 80-year-old Bob Hope again doing a Christmas show for a GI audience in a tense military zone had to stir patriotic feelings in the viewer, no matter what the individual's stance on the present Lebanon danger zone. Hope has always been at his best in front of some distant enthusiastic audience, as if the challenge of getting there in the first place has got all of his comic juices going. . . .
>
> The content was the same as always . . . but the focus was mostly on Hope. . . . One could not help but assume that some of the sailor jokes dated back two or three wars, but no matter – the troops loved it as they always have. Hope seemed to fumble his lines more than usual (exec producer Hope left all that in), but mostly it was the world's best-known comedian doing his thing one more time for a highly appreciable [sic] audience.
>
> One could not help feel that the seemingly indestructible Hope represented, once again, that individuality of purpose that only the American mystique seems to generate – and that the US would persevere as it always has, bumbles and all.[1]

Among other tasks that month, Hope headlined a fund-raiser for the New York Hospital–Cornell Medical Center, helping raise $1 million.

In February, Bob and Dolores celebrated their fiftieth wedding anniversary. A fiftieth wedding anniversary is a proud accomplishment, and when the couple has lived in Hollywood in the public eye for most of that time, it's really something special.

Reporters asked Bob what he gave Dolores on this momentous occasion and he told them he had given her what she really wanted: he had gone to Mass with her. He also presented his beautiful wife with a diamond necklace. Bob wanted a big party in Palm Springs, but Dolores convinced him to have a quiet dinner for two in their North Hollywood home. Hope told the press he was looking forward to the next big event – their seventy-fifth anniversary!

His TV special that month was a spoof of the current crop of TV shows. Later, he took time to comment about some of television's most popular stars. Following the announcement that Jackie Gleason's 'Honeymooners' was being brought back on Showtime, the pay cable service, Hope spoke about his long-time friend and golfing buddy. 'I love everything he's ever done. I was thrilled to hear there would be more "Honeymooners" revived.'[2]

Speaking of Bill Cosby, Hope said *The Cosby Show* was a 'standout' and that he admired the way the comedian handled his series. 'He doesn't overdo. He's so bright.'[3]

Commenting on younger comedians, Hope said that one of the obstacles they face is that they don't travel enough to find out what people like. '(George) Burns and I were talking about it the other night at my Palm Springs home. Jack Benny, Fred Allen, Burns and Allen, myself – we all played theatres around the country. A month here, a month there. We found out what people wanted, what they thought, and we tested their reactions. Today, comedians take the easy way out – they get dirty. They don't have to dig for material as we did. Before I could afford writers, I picked up jokes everywhere.'[4]

That method certainly seems to have worked for Bob Hope.

There was no shortage of honours, especially Ivy League honours, in 1984. On 30 March, he received an honorary degree of Doctor of Humane Letters from Columbia University in New York for his contributions to the Children's Tumor Clinic at the Edward S. Harkness Eye Institute of Columbia-Presbyterian

Medical Center. Hope has remained active in supporting and encouraging the blind ever since his first trouble with his own eyes.

In early April, Hope taught four classes at Southern Methodist University in Texas. As Distinguished Visiting Professor of Comedy, he held forth in the auditorium he paid for on the subject of one-liners, gags and monologues.

In May, Hope celebrated his eighty-first birthday with another TV special, this time from New Orleans. Hope said when they lit the candles on his birthday cake during the taping of the show that all the smoke alarms in New Orleans would go off. Stars who helped him celebrate his birthday included John Ritter, Johnny Cash, Placido Domingo, Sugar Ray Leonard, Brooke Shields, 'Mr T', Marvin Hagler, David Letterman, Red Buttons and of course, Dolores. Dolores' song in 1984 was 'I'll String Along with You'.

On 6 May, he was presented with the Distinguished Public Service Award from the students at Princeton.

Once again, Hope was asked how he kept himself so young. He said, 'By never being bored. When people ask me what my outlook is, I say, "Do something you enjoy and stay in there pitching." I never get bored with my work. There's always something new. And there's nothing like pleasing an audience.'[5]

Hope continued performing and preparing TV specials through the summer. In September his sponsor Texaco took out a full page ad in *Variety*. Under a Hirschfeld caricature of the famous face, the copy read:

> Congratulations, Bob.
> For us at Texaco, the highlight of this Sunday evening's Emmy Awards will be when Bob Hope steps up to receive the highest honour the Academy of Television Arts & Sciences can bestow, the Governors Award.
> According to the Academy, the Governors Award is presented for "outstanding achievement that is [so] extraordinary and universal in nature as to be beyond the scope of the Emmy Awards." For us here at Texaco, where this year we're celebrating Bob Hope's tenth anniversary as our spokesman, that description of the Governors Award is a model of understatement.[6]

At last Bob Hope had an Emmy.

On 28 September 1984, Hope marked his thirty-fifth anniversary with NBC with another special, entitled, 'Bob Hope Presents the Hilarious Unrehearsed Antics of the Stars', cashing in on the current trend for TV bloopers. The programme was about embarrassing moments or 'bloopers' that Hope used to collect and show on Johnny Carson's *Tonight Show* when he appeared to tout his latest special. The show marked Hope's seventh five-year deal with NBC, his original network.

He was already looking forward to his tour the following month in Britain, having received a letter from a man who said he had pictures of the house where Bob's parents had lived in Wales. Bob decided to do the performances in the UK and take the opportunity to go and see this part of his family history.

Off the 81-year-old went for an eight-day, six-city tour. He flew over by Concorde and played the next day to rapturous audiences. Standing ovations greeted both his entrance on stage and his exits, the show in between lasting nearly an hour.

While in England, Hope experienced one of the most ironic incidents of his long career. After so many shows presented in the midst of war, he was forced to cancel his show in peaceful Portsmouth when construction workers unearthed a 550-pound German bomb from World War II which had lain buried under the theatre. No terrorist act, it was a leftover, but even after lying in wait for 40 years, it was still dangerous. The people who wanted to see Hope could not be allowed near the site.

The rest of the tour, however, went very well, and Bob travelled to Wales and saw his parents' home.

Once back in the US, Bob heard the results of a Louis Harris Poll. Bob Hope, leading a list that included Richard Pryor, Eddie Murphy, Bill Cosby and Red Skelton, was the People's Choice as America's Favourite Comedian, winning by a wide margin.

Bob Hope can even make news by *not* making the news. The London *Times* published a report on 19 September 1984, that Hope had *not* made the list of the 400 richest Americans.

Although Hope would rather not read about his personal finances in the press, he could open the October edition of *Forbes* magazine to find the headline, 'How Rich Is Bob Hope?' The year before, *Forbes* had concluded that his net worth was over $200 million. Hope had protested, stating that his estate was worth far less than that, though he didn't specify any exact amount.

The magazine had hired real estate appraisers and financial wizards who concluded that Hope's real estate, centred mostly in California, was worth about $85 million at the day's prices. Other holdings were estimated at $30 million more. His income annually for television shows, commercials, endorsements and stage performances was estimated at about $3 million or more.

In December, Hope's Christmas special found him back in home territory. He was glad there was no trouble spot that needed his services.

Hope's thirty-fifth Christmas special was very different from the one the year before on the battleships off Beirut. This time he was performing in comfort, along with Shirley Jones and Mary Lou Retton.

Hope's TV specials continue. Some of us enjoy watching because we really laugh at the humour, others have more nostalgic reasons, and still others are attracted because Bob Hope is such an institution. John J. O'Connor, the *New York Times* critic, said not long ago:

> There is . . . the phenomenon of Bob Hope, who was back on NBC . . . with still another of his Hope Enterprises specials. . . .
> By now, after some 35 years on television, the Hope formula is set in Krazy Glue. An opening monologue, keyed to timely news items, is followed by a series of sketches that will find Mr Hope and his guests in an assortment of silly costumes and wigs, prompting the performers to giggle at themselves periodically. Memorizing lines is still not one of the show's priorities. The eyes of Mr Hope and company are nearly always glued to cue cards off camera. But no matter. The comedian and his loyal fans are clearly comfortable with one another. It is not, at this point, a terribly demanding relationship. . . .
> [As] always, his humor is basically gentle, almost supportive. . . . Perhaps like George Burns, one of the few guests who can call him 'Junior', Mr Hope transcends the ordinary criteria for comedy.[7]

Bob Hope and George Burns have virtually created new careers out of joking about their ages, although Hope does it less than Burns. They also get comic material out of each other. In reference to the fact that Reagan is the oldest American President in history, yet much younger than Burns, Hope says, 'George Burns is thinking of running for President. He worries that it's dangerous to have a kid running the country.' Burns turned 89 in January 1985, and Hope said, 'He's just signed a new contract in Vegas for five years . . . with options'.[8]

George Burns easily gets back at Hope. 'Bob Hope will live to be a hundred – if he's booked,' Burns says.[9]

Both men performed at a benefit in Palm Springs for the Eisenhower Medical Center. The tickets were $5,000 per couple, or $25,000 if one attended the cocktail party at Walter Annenberg's. Hope said, 'It was the first benefit I'd ever heard of that was listed on the New York Stock Exchange. I was late to the cocktail party and only had one glass of champagne. That worked out to $2,000 a bubble.'[10]

In an article in *The Times*[11] in 1985, Charles Champlin reported on a week in the life of Bob Hope. Hope played nine holes of golf in the Andy Williams Open in San Diego, flew on to Tulsa to work a Children's Care Center benefit, zoomed over to Little Rock, Arkansas, for a banquet, on to Orlando the next morning for a hotel dedication, and then the following morning went to Sun City, Arizona for a rehearsal in the morning, a performance in the afternoon, and then a flight the next morning back to Los Angeles to start another week. It would be an incredible schedule for a man half his age!

For his eighty-second birthday television special in May, 1985, Hope returned to England. Appearing on the show was Prince Philip. The entertainers, a broad spectrum of stars, included Lord Laurence Olivier, Brooke Shields, Julio Iglesias, Bernadette Peters, Charlton Heston, Debbie Reynolds, Phyllis Diller, Crystal Gayle and Duran Duran. Michael Caine, who received the cheque from Bob and was president so many years ago of the boys' club run by little Reverend Butterworth, was on hand. Back then Caine had been known as Maurice Mickelwhite. Hope said if he'd known the boy would become so successful, he would have adopted him.

The TV event was done as a benefit for Prince Philip's programme for young people. Dolores was on hand, and serenaded her husband for his birthday. Her song for this show was 'I've Grown Accustomed to His Face'.

One sign of Bob Hope's stature, not only in the world of entertainment but in the world at large, is that on a September 1985 TV special, he had cameo appearances by Gerald Ford, George Burns, Ted Turner (owner of three cable TV services, the Atlanta Braves, and now MGM), Lee Iacocca of Chrysler, Johnny Carson and President Ronald Reagan. They were joined by guest stars Danny Thomas, Lynda Carter, Milton Berle and 'Mr T'.

Not all was rosy for Bob in 1985, however. He lost the last of his brothers, Fred C. Hope, who died in Cleveland at the age of 87. Fred had run the meat business that gave Bob a part-time job so long ago when he was dreaming of vaudeville.

Bob Hope has received five special Academy Awards. In 1949, he received a silver plaque for service to the entertainment industry. In 1944, he had been awarded lifetime membership in the Academy, and in 1952 he was given a statue for service to the industry and the nation. The year 1959 saw him honoured with the Jean Hersholt Humanitarian Award and in 1965 he received the first gold medal for service to the industry and the nation, having just received the Governors Award at the 'Emmy' ceremony.

Now, he was to receive the highest award an entertainer can get. In December 1985, Bob Hope joined with lyricist-playwright Alan Jay Lerner, composer Frederick Loewe, actress Irene Dunne, dancer-choreographer Merce Cunningham and opera star and administrator Beverly Sills to receive the Kennedy Center Honors.

The evening began with a White House reception hosted by Ronald and Nancy Reagan. The President said, 'Each of you has made life a happier thing for all of us. You have enhanced life – you've made it more fun. You've moved us and made us laugh, made us cheer, and made our souls soar as you soared. . .'

Walter Cronkite was master of ceremonies at the Kennedy Center. Each of the honourees was specially remembered, although the *New York Times* had this to say of the evening:

> . . . Perhaps the high note of the weekend's festivities was the closing of this evening's performance when 120 servicemen – members of the Soldiers' Chorus, the Navy Sea Chanters, the 82d Airborne Chorus and the Fife and Drum Corps – gathered on stage to salute Mr Hope in song, ending with "Thanks for the Memory". From their ranks,

eight men and one woman identified themselves and recalled a moment on the battlefield – Guadalcanal in 1944, Sicily in 1944, the Carrier Essex in 1943, Korea in 1951 and Da Nang in 1967 – when Mr Hope and members of his USO troupe dropped into their midst with a message from home.[12]

Hope wore his medal with pride.

The honour meant that Bob could now sit back and rest on his laurels; if he wanted, he could retire. Bob Hope wouldn't hear of it.

In 1985, he took on a new civic responsibility in joining the 47-member Ellis Island Commission, which was preparing for the 100th anniversary of the Statue of Liberty. Also on the commission were such luminaries as Matthew Ridgeway, William Westmoreland and Lionel Hampton.

Also in that year, Hope signed up for the 'Crafted With Pride' advertising campaign encouraging Americans to purchase goods made in the USA. He continues to make television specials and give live performances. As if that were not enough, he decided to do something new, and made his first television movie.

Broadcast on 27 January 1986, the movie was called *A Masterpiece of Murder* and starred Hope and Don Ameche. Hope portrayed Dan Dolan, a down-at-the-heels gum-shoe who finds himself at the same party with Frank Aherne, played by Ameche. Thirty years before, Hope had arrested Ameche for burglary, but now Ameche was very well off. The host of the party is murdered and Hope and Ameche join forces to solve the murder. Needless to say, there are more one-liners than clues.

Other celebrities in the movie included Kevin McCarthy, Stella Stevens, Jayne Meadows, Frank Gorshin, Anne Francis, Anita Morris, Yvonne DeCarlo, and Jamie Farr (playing himself).

Bob Hope's fans can only hope that the comedian will be around for a good many years to come. Listening to the man himself, one can't help thinking that it's a sure thing, because not only does he have the secret of long life, but apparently the secret of youth. In the spring of 1985 he wrote:

> If I were asked, "To what do you attribute your good health?" I'd answer, exercise (golf), keep active (work) and watch my diet (if I don't, Dolores does).

But of equal importance to my happiness and health are involvement with people and being able to laugh and thankfully, make others laugh.

It's been said laughter is an instant vacation. True. Fun is good medicine with healing power. Laughter is a tonic. . . .

Laughing or creating laughter – is as important as any medicine and costs absolutely nothing.

Entertaining GIs in three wars, I have seen the healing power of laughter and I can still see it. . . . I remember entertaining at a mental hospital. "I'd like to sing a little song for you," I said, "but I need music. Can anyone in the audience play 'Buttons and Bows?'"

"Yes," the patients yelled, "Charlie can."

Charlie played the piano with one finger while I sang. A month later I got a letter from a doctor at the hospital that read:

"I thought you'd like to know Charlie was one of the worst cases we've ever had. But from the day you brought him up on stage and made him smile, he has improved. We think he'll now eventually lead a normal life. . . ".

Fun combats problems of ageing. It is a stimulant that enables us to rise to challenges. My former neighbour, Walt Disney, worked almost obsessively. . . . Yet despite Walt's hard work, when he was asked to sum up the secret of his success, he replied, "Fun."

But you don't have to be Bob Hope or Walt Disney to have fun bringing fun to others.[13]

Epilogue

There are but a handful of individuals in the world whose names immediately suggest what their lives are all about and their impact upon the rest of us.

The first majority of 'power names' are those of presidents, princes and potentates who govern and shape our lives. The next category for instant recognition are the discoverers and inventors who alter the way we go about our lives.

Finally, there are the handful who make us laugh or cry and, in either case, help us escape the problems and pressures of our everyday lives.

There are literally tens of thousands of actors who hold fourth on the stages of the world in person or electronically. Most don't make a living. A few become successful. A very, very few are really remembered. In any generation one or two become such an important part of our lives that when those funny lists are assembled of the 'most admired' or 'best liked', an actor's name will often precede a prime minister's.

Hold up a magnifying glass and the jokes are not all that different from others who try to make us laugh. The man himself is certainly not particularly pretty, so the magic can't be what we see. Yet, each time he goes before an audience, regardless of their language or their lifestyle, he finds a way to have fun with his uncanny sense of timing and the little smile that's all his own and which makes us forget our problems.

Hope's magic has worked on the battlefields of the world for troops of many nations when he brought shows to those who could enjoy only minutes away from combat. It works in the sometimes antiseptic world of television and even works over radio, when only the voice and not the 'look' reaches his audience.

James Hope was an artisan who went to France to help carve the Statue of Liberty. His grandson, Bob Hope, went to America to carve a career that would touch the lives of audiences throughout the world.

Between laughs Bob Hope plays golf with presidents of the United States, is honoured by royalty and collects honorary degrees and other awards as frequently as some men buy new suits.

No matter where Hope appears throughout the world, the band always strikes up his familiar signature song, 'Thanks For The Memory.'

Thank *you*, Bob.

Sources

Chapter 2
1. W. R. Faith, *Bob Hope, A Life In Comedy* (New York, C. P. Putnam's Sons, 1982), p. 45

Chapter 5
1. *Good Housekeeping*, July 1982
2. Bob Hope, as told to Dwayne Netland, *Confessions of a Hooker, My Life-long Love Affair with Golf* (New York, Doubleday, 1985), p. 135
3. W. R. Faith, *Bob Hope, A Life in Comedy* (New York, C. P. Putnam's Sons, 1982), p. 154
4. *Ibid*. p. 176

Chapter 6
1. W. R. Faith, *Bob Hope, A Life in Comedy* (New York, C. P. Putnam's Sons, 1982), pp. 247–8

Chapter 7
1. *TV Guide*, Jan 16–22, 1965
2. Leonard Maltin (ed), *TV Movies* (New York, New American Library, 1982), p. 218
3. *Ibid*.

Chapter 8
1. *People*, 15.1.1979, p. 75
2. *Village Voice*, 28.5.1979, p. 38
3. *Reader's Digest*, March 1981, p. 179
4. *Variety*, 27.5.1981, p. 54
5. *Ibid*.
6. *Village Voice*, 4.11.1981, p. 61

Chapter 9
1. *Saturday Evening Post*, Oct 1981
2. *TV Guide*, 21.5.1983
3. *Ibid.*
4. *Ladies Home Journal*, June 1983, p.144
5. *Observer*, 14.10.1984
6. *New York Daily News*, 25.5.1981
7. *People*, 15.1.1969

Chapter 10
1. Bob Hope, as told to Dwayne Netland, *Confessions of a Hooker, My Life-long Love Affair with Golf* (New York, Doubleday, 1985)
2. *Ibid.* p. 55
3. *Ibid.* p. 22
4. *Ibid.* p. 47
5. *Ibid.* p. 18
6. *Ibid.* p. 25
7. *Ibid.*

Chapter 11
1. Charles Thompson, *Bob Hope, Portrait of a Superstar* (New York, St Martin's Press, 1981), p. 94
2. *Ibid.* p. 95
3. *New York Daily News*, 3.5.1984
4. Charles Thompson, *Bob Hope, Portrait of a Superstar* (New York, St Martin's Press, 1981), p. 204

Chapter 12
1. W. R. Faith, *Bob Hope, A Life In Comedy* (New York, C. P. Putnam's Sons, 1982), p. 258
2. *People*, 15.1.1979, p. 76
3. *TV Guide*, 21.5.1983
4. *Ibid.*

Chapter 14
1. W. R. Faith, *Bob Hope, A Life In Comedy* (New York, C. P. Putnam's Sons, 1982), p. 27
2. *TV Guide*, 21.5.1983
3. *Ibid.*

Chapter 15
1. Bob Thomas, *The One and Only Bing* (New York, Grosset and Dunlap, 1977), p. 151
2. *Ibid.* p. 62
3. Bob Hope and Bob Thomas, *The Road to Hollywood, My 40-Year Love Affair with the Movies* (New York, Doubleday, 1977, pp. 32–3
4. Bob Thomas, *The One and Only Bing* (New York, Grosset and Dunlap, 1977)
5. Robert Bookbinder, *The Films of Bing Crosby* (Secaucus, New Jersey, The Citadel Press, 1977), p. 27
6. *Ibid.* p. 36
7. *Ibid.* p. 108
8. Bob Hope and Bob Thomas, *The Road to Hollywood, My 40-Year Love Affair with the Movies* (New York, Doubleday, 1977), p. 42
9. *Ibid.* p. 43
10. *Ibid.* p. 42
11. *Ibid.* p. 43
12. Robert Bookbinder, *The Films of Bing Crosby* (Secaucus, New Jersey, The Citadel Press, 1977), p. 31
13. *Ibid.* pp. 245–6
14. *Ibid.* p. 246
15. Bob Hope, as told to Dwayne Netland, *Confessions of a Hooker, My Life-long Love Affair with Golf* New York, Doubleday, 1985), p. 150

Chapter 16
1. Bob Hope, as told to Peter Martin, *The Last Christmas Show* (New York, Doubleday, 1974), p. 6
2. W. R. Faith, *Bob Hope, A Life in Comedy* (New York, C. P. Putnam's Sons, 1982), p. 169
3. *Ibid.* p. 180
4. *Ibid.* pp. 326–7
5. *Ibid.*
6. Charles Thompson, *Bob Hope, Portrait of a Superstar* (New York, St Martin's Press, 1981), p. 146
7. *Ibid.* p. 6

Chapter 17
 1. *Variety*, 18.1.1984, p. 50
 2. *New York Daily News*, 22.2.1984
 3. *Ibid.*
 4. *Ibid.*
 5. *New York Daily News*, 28.5.1984
 6. *Variety*, 19.9.1984, p. 109
 7. *New York Times*, 26.2.1985
 8. *The Times*, 21.2.1985
 9. *Ibid.*
10. *Ibid.*
11. *Ibid.*
12. *New York Times*, 9.12.1985
13. *Connections*, Spring 1985, pp. 8–9

Index

Within entries Bob Hope is referred to by the initials BH